D1522923

give us today ou.
DAILY BREAD
OCTOBER/NOVEMBER/DECEMBER 2023

C O N T E N T S

Sarah Magardician

Authors

Yvonne Lee (Proverbs 1:1-9:18)
Joy King (Jeremiah 1-9)
Jason Perry (Jeremiah 10-17)
Paul Lee (Joshua 15-22)
Dennis Miller (Joshua 23-24; Isaiah 54:1-8)
Paul Chang (Luke 20:19-24:53)
Jacob Kim (Psalm 100; Proverbs 10-12)
Tony King (Proverbs 13-16)
Joe Wert (Jeremiah 18-28)
David Miller (Luke 1:5-2:14)

Editors

Grace Baik
Esther Kim
John Lee

October

Mon	Tue	Wed	Thu	Fri	Sat	Sun
						1
2	3	4	5	6	7	8
9	10	11	12	13	14	15
16	17	18	19	20	21	22
23	24	25	26	27	28	29
30	31					

INTRODUCTION TO PROVERBS

Proverbs, for the most part, was written by King Solomon. When Solomon became king, he did not ask for wealth and power; he asked God to give him wisdom so that he could be a good shepherd for God's people. God was pleased and gave him wisdom--and power and wealth as well (2Ch 1:7-12).

The Proverbs reflect his wisdom. (Solomon himself did not follow his own advice; he gave his heart to many foreign wives and sowed the seed of idolatry among his people [1Ki 11:8; Ne 13:26]).

A proverb is a short, wise statement that expresses some truth about human behavior. The wisdom of Solomon taught in this book is not just good advice based on human common sense. It rests on the fear of God. He says in 9:10, "The fear of the Lord is the beginning of wisdom."

The stated purpose of the book is to help young people "acquire a disciplined and prudent life by doing what is right and just and fair." It is to give "prudence to the simple, knowledge and discretion to the young" and to add to the knowledge of the wise. The first 9 chapters are directed to young men and warn about the temptations of money and immoral women. In these chapters, Wisdom and Folly are personified. The rewards of following the way of wisdom, and the consequences of following the way of folly are well defined.

THE FEAR OF THE LORD

Proverbs 1:1-7
Key Verse 1:7

This passage introduces the theme of Proverbs. It was written by King Solomon, David's successor, who asked God for wisdom to shepherd his people. God blessed him with wisdom, and he was known as the wisest man on earth. Solomon shares his godly wisdom in Proverbs.

Godly wisdom helps us to live prudent and righteous lives. We need godly wisdom to be able to rise above our sinful nature and worldly trends and ideologies. The simple tend to be young people who are wide open in their minds and hearts. Without wisdom, they can fall into a pit or trap. The simple need prudence to channel their lives and to behave in a right and just way. Godly wisdom protects people to live discreetly.

If you don't know what to do, study Proverbs to gain wisdom. Those who are wise can add to their wisdom. Those who are discerning can have keener insight. We all – young and old – need wisdom. The secret to and beginning of wisdom is the fear of God. Then, when we fear God and honor God as God in our lives, we can have his Spirit to guide us with wisdom. The mark of a fool is that he despises godly wisdom and instruction. The fool follows his own faulty understanding and thinks he knows what is best.

Prayer: Father, thank you for giving us wisdom when we fear you and seek from you what is right.

One Word: Fear God and receive wisdom.

LISTEN TO GOD AND LIVE

Proverbs 1:8-33
Key Verse 1:33

Solomon advises his son (and us) against acquiring immoral earnings (v. 15). Not all of us may be engaging in ambushing and looting as in this passage, but we should all examine our hearts to see if "precious substance" (v. 13 KJV) is a stumbling block as we follow Christ, as Jesus said, "You cannot serve both God and money" (Matthew 6:26). Love of material gain will eventually cost us our lives (v. 19), piercing us with many griefs (1 Timothy 6:10). We should not justify our crafty ways.

Solomon fiercely rebukes us to repent our stubbornness and foolishness. He points out that we are pushing away God's wisdom while childishly indulging ourselves with our pride. He warns us that this behavior brings calamities like a storm, one after another. Our lives without the fear of God will be conquered by constant stress and anxiety.

We must desire God's knowledge and learn to reject our selfish thoughts. We must open our ears to listen to God's voice and calling. Then God will bless us with his eternal safety and comfort.

Prayer: Father, thank you for giving us your wisdom. When I am tempted by dishonest gain, help me to listen to you and live a blessed life.

One Word: Listen to God and live.

THE VALUE OF WISDOM

Proverbs 2:1-22
Key Verse 2:6

The Bible is a perennial steady seller. But only people who seek and search for it as a hidden treasure (4) find wisdom. Whoever finds wisdom, wisdom protects them and guards their course (8). Wisdom will save them from the ways of wicked men who have left the straight paths, who delight in doing wrong, whose paths are crooked, and who are devious in their ways (12-15).

If we accept wisdom, then we will understand what is right, just, and fair -- every good path. For wisdom will enter our heart, and knowledge will be pleasant to our soul (10) like the true vine and the branches (John 15:5).

If we seek wisdom, we will walk in the ways of the good and live in the land (20, 21). But the wicked will be cut off from the land (22).

Prayer: Father, thank you for giving me wisdom, knowledge and understanding. Help me to store them up in my heart and repent my wickedness.

One Word: Value and seek God's wisdom.

TRUST IN THE LORD WITH ALL YOUR HEART

Proverbs 3:1-10
Key Verse 3:5

Solomon urges us to practice God's love to those around us, and to be faithful in any circumstance. In the midst of our busy lives, it is very easy to forget about God. We often tend to drift away from God to gain control over our own lives. We often think that we understand ourselves better than God and therefore attempt to rely on our own accomplishments.

However, human strength always fails. We must endlessly depend on God and his almighty power. We must fear the Lord and ask for his guidance in our lives. When we finally surrender ourselves completely to God, he will bless us and make our paths straight.

Our Creator God knows exactly what we need and provides everything out of his power and love. Only God can be the truest nourishment to our souls. Let's trust in God with all our ways, surrendering to him my own stubborn ideas and plans.

Prayer: Father, thank you for giving me your wisdom. Help me to trust in you with all my heart and lean not on my own understanding.

One Word: Trust in the Lord with all your heart.

BLESSED IS THE ONE WHO FINDS WISDOM

Proverbs 3:11-26
Key Verse 3:12

Wisdom involves discipline. God disciplines those he loves. We should not despise God's discipline. A good father disciplines his children to teach them the right way to go. Our Father God, in his wisdom, disciplines us for our own good out of his love to raise us in the right way. We should not despise God's discipline but thank him for it. Are you guilty of despising the Lord's discipline? Repent and thank him for his love and wisdom to help you.

When we grow in wisdom, we are truly blessed. We become truly rich in understanding — which profits our lives far more than rare jewels. Having godly wisdom is compared to the tree of life in the Garden of Eden (18). With wisdom, understanding, and knowledge, God created the heavens and earth. (19-20) If we base our lives on godly wisdom, understanding, and knowledge, we will have a firm foundation. Wisdom gives life to our souls (22).

Many things in life make us stumble and fall. We are confused, afraid, and helpless. But having wisdom makes our way secure, so that we are no longer afraid, and our sleep is sweet. We are confident in the Lord who will protect us.

Prayer: Father, thank you for disciplining me according to your wisdom so that I may live a truly blessed life.

One Word: Seek God's wisdom and be blessed.

WISDOM IN DEALING WITH PEOPLE

Proverbs 3:27-35
Key Verse 3:35

An area of our life that truly requires wisdom is our relationships with people. This passage gives us proverbs to help us to have wisdom in dealing with people. Many times, we fail to have wisdom in our relationships and succumb to our feelings, temptations, and pride. We need to pray and ask for wisdom, and God will help us (Ja 1:5).

How we treat our neighbor requires wisdom. We should assist our neighbor within our power to do so (27). We should not do anything evil to our neighbor, betraying their trust. We should give generously and freely to our neighbors instead of avoiding them when they need help.

We shouldn't fight with others for petty reasons. We should not envy violent people who abuse others to get their own way. We should know that those who are wicked are cursed, but the righteous are indeed blessed. God lifts up the humble and scorns the proud (34). God honors those who act wisely in their relationships with others. Are you struggling with others? Ask God for his wisdom to act honorably and be blessed by him.

Prayer: Father, thank you for giving me wisdom on how to interact with people. Please help me to be wise and honorable, trusting you to bless me.

One Word: Be wise and honorable in my relationships with people.

GET WISDOM AND GET UNDERSTANDING

Proverbs 4:1-9
Key Verse 4:7

The writer (King Solomon) reminds the readers that he was a son of his father (King David). And his father taught him (3). And he wants to teach us the same topic.

"Take hold of my words with all your heart; keep my commands, and you will live. Get wisdom, get understanding; … Do not forsake wisdom, and she will protect you; … Get wisdom. Though it costs all you have, get understanding." (4-9)

To seek and keep wisdom, we encounter risks from time to time. But this proverb encourages us to seek and keep wisdom though it costs all we have. Why? Because wisdom will exalt us, honor us, and present us with a glorious crown. It will be like treasure hidden in a field and a merchant looking to find pearls (Mt 13:44, 45).

Prayer: Father, thank you for your teachings that bless my life. Help me to get wisdom and insight above all things.

One Word: Above all, get wisdom and insight.

TWO WAYS

Proverbs 4:10-27
Key Verse 4:11

This passage compares and contrasts two ways. The first way is to accept wise instruction and to follow it. When we humbly accept instruction, we will be upright in heart. We will have spirit and strength to run our race by faith. By diligently following the right way, we can guard ourselves from the consequences of sin and wickedness.

We must decide not to follow the way of evil and wickedness. When we are tempted, we must avoid it, turn away from it, and do not go near it. Wickedness controls us so that we cannot sleep unless we satisfy its wicked desires. We become evil and violent. We are no longer ourselves.

To overcome this, we must listen to what is right and keep God's commands in our hearts. They will bring us life and healing. We must be alert and guard our path to go the right way with a fear of God, holiness, and the courage to do what is right. We must ponder our ways (26) and honestly ask ourselves, what way am I following? Am I seeking God's way or my own evil desires?

Prayer: Father, thank you for showing me the way of life in Jesus. Please help me to follow his teachings and live by faith in him.

One Word: Follow the right way.

DRINK WATER FROM YOUR OWN CISTERN

Proverbs 5:1-23
Key Verse 5:15

Proverbs 5 strongly warns against <u>sexual immorality.</u>

First, we must use <u>discretion in our speech and guard our lips.</u> The path to sexual immorality begins with who we associate with and choose to talk to. By opening this door, we make ourselves susceptible to smooth talk or a line that hooks us into an immoral relationship. Next, we are trapped by where we go and with whom. We would not fall into immorality if we did not go alone somewhere with the opposite sex. (This includes being alone with a digital device for sexual pleasure.) After committing sexual immorality, what is the result? Tragically, lives are ruined (9-14). Immorality makes us lose everything: our strength, spirit, power, wealth, and reputation.

Second, we must reserve sex for marriage. The command, "Drink water from your own cistern," is a metaphor meaning that sex was made for marriage. There is an intoxicating joy in marital sex. <u>Complete intimacy with your marriage partner brings real love and delight.</u> It is a fountain of blessing to us. To achieve marital purity, we must fear God who sees all our ways and be on guard against the snares of folly and cords of sin.

Prayer: Father, thank you for your strong warning against sexual immorality. Please help me to have discretion and guard my ways before you.

One Word: : <u>Let your fountain be blessed (18).</u>

FREE YOURSELF

Proverbs 6:1-11
Key Verse 6:5

Often without wisdom, we agree too hastily to a commitment that we cannot keep or will burden us too much. When we realize that we have done so, we must not sleep until we have freed ourselves. We will regret it if we do not. The financial, physical, mental, and emotional toll will be our undoing.

The author of the proverb gives two analogies of freedom: a gazelle from the hand of the hunter and a bird from the trap of the fowler. It is highly unlikely that either can get free, but it's possible when they try persistently with all their strength. To succeed, the trapped prey doesn't give up until they have escaped, even if they are injured and bleeding.

Why do people not seek a way out from their unwise commitments? It is because they procrastinate or are too lazy to try. Those who sleep and try to forget about it will lose precious opportunities and become impoverished. The proverb offers the example of an ant, which is so diligent and self-starting. Though so small, an ant displays extraordinary commitment, diligence, patience, planning, work ethic, and wisdom.

Prayer: Father, thank you for giving me the means to get out of any situation when I persistently do something by faith. Help me to escape unwise commitments before it is too late.

One Word: Be diligent and be free.

KEEP GOD'S COMMANDS IN YOUR HEART

Proverbs 6:12-35
Key Verse 6:21

People will always try to deceive and trick you. Beware of sly and adulterous people who tempt you to follow their ways. Rather, remember the wise teachings of our spiritual parents to do what is upright and godly. We should imprint God's commands on our hearts and follow them as our inner light. We need to meditate on them day and night, and this will guide us and keep us from falling astray. We will open our eyes to see scams and traps around us and avoid them.

The proverb gives a strong warning especially against adultery. It seems so common. Yet, when people commit adultery, it's like scooping fire into one's lap. Reputations are ruined, and the stigma of shame is never removed. Moreover, a jealous spouse will oppose you, punish you, and never forget. Who wants to live in a firepit like this?

Passion makes people blind and careless in their choices. It steals their hearts and minds and makes them sick with lust. Those who follow their adulterous desires and break up a family will have to live with this great shame for the rest of their lives as a testament against them. Even years later, David was still remembered for committing adultery with Bathsheba (Mt 1:6).

Prayer: Father, thank you for your laws protecting me. Help me to imprint your righteous commands on my heart and be on guard against adultery.

One Word: Bind God's laws on your heart.

THE APPLE OF YOUR EYE

Proverbs 7:1-27
Key Verse 7:2

This proverb is another strong warning against adultery. The best way to avoid adultery is to treasure God's commands – not sex and beauty. We need to keep God's commands and obey them, and to keep God's words as the apple of my eye. What we seek and desire as the apple of our eye will dictate our actions and the direction of our lives. What is the apple of your eye?

Verses 6-23 describe a man swooped up in adultery. He is captivated by the adulteress' smooth talk and goes where he should not go (near her corner, the road to her house) when he should not (twilight, evening, darkness). She runs out to meet him in the street and brazenly kisses him in public. She tells him that he is special. She promises him delicious food (sacrifices) and a romantic rendezvous, and she assures him that their secret will be secure. Using her seductive powers, she leads him into sin. Once he follows her, he is trapped by his own desire.

It would be wise to not pay any attention to the seductress in the first place. If a man doesn't talk to her or listen to her, she doesn't have a chance. Throughout history, the adulterous woman is like a mighty warrior who has slain hordes of men.

Prayer: Father, thank you for giving us a clear warning about adultery. Help me to keep your commands as the apple of my eye.

One Word: What is the apple of my eye?

WISDOM'S CALL

Proverbs 8:1-21
Key Verse 8:11

At the highest point along the way, where the paths meet, wisdom takes her stand; beside the gate leading into the city, at the entrance, she cries aloud: "To you, O people, I call out; I raise my voice to all mankind. You who are simple, gain prudence; you who are foolish, set your hearts on it." (4,5) Wisdom is calling out to us. Are we listening?

Rubies are rarer and more valuable than diamonds. Wisdom is more precious than rubies, and nothing we desire can compare with her (11). Whoever seeks wisdom even though he is simple and foolish, finds her (17). By wisdom, kings reign. By wisdom, princes govern.

Wisdom will give us prudence which means the way (5). Wisdom will speak what is true and what is just (7, 8). Finally, wisdom gives us better than fine gold (19) - life. Jesus answered, "I am the way and the truth and the life." (John 14:6)

Prayer: Thank you, Lord, for wisdom. Please open my eyes and heart to seek wisdom.

One Word: Listen to and seek for wisdom.

WISDOM WAS WITH GOD IN THE BEGINNING

Proverbs 8:22-36
Key Verse 8:23

Wisdom was formed long ago, at the very beginning, when the world came to be (23). Wisdom says she was before the world (24-29). After creation, she was constantly at his side and rejoicing always in his presence, rejoicing in his whole world, and delighting in mankind (30, 31). These verses remind us of the verse "God saw all that he had made, and it was very good." (Ge1:31)

These verses also remind us of John's gospel; "In the beginning was the Word, and the Word was with God, and the Word was God. He was with God in the beginning." (Jn 1:1-3)

This Wisdom, the Creator, will bless us if we keep his ways, if we listen to his instruction, and if we find wisdom (32-35).

Prayer: Lord, who rejoiced after creation, help me follow your wisdom.

One Word: I will follow wisdom.

INVITATIONS OF WISDOM AND FOLLY

Proverbs 9:1-18
Key Verse 9:10

In this passage, there are two invitations, one from wisdom (1-6), and another from an unruly woman (13-18). The consequence for each invitation is very different (7-12).

Wisdom has built her house and set up its seven pillars. She prepared a meal and wine and invited people even who had no sense, "Come, eat my food and drink the wine. And leave your simple ways and you will live; walk in the way of insight." Wisdom will reward you!

Folly sits at the door of her house, on a seat at the highest point of the city, calling out to those who pass by, "Let all who are simple come to my house! Stolen water is sweet; food eaten in secret is delicious!" Her guests are deep in the realm of the dead. Folly will kill you!

Only wisdom will give us life and insight. The fear of the Lord is the beginning of wisdom (10). Jesus also invites us, "Let anyone who is thirsty come to me and drink." (John 7:37-38).

Prayer: Thank you, Lord, for your invitation even though I am simple. Lord, open my eyes and ears to accept your invitation.

One Word: Wisdom will reward you.

INTRODUCTION TO JEREMIAH

Jeremiah served Jerusalem and Judah as a prophet for 40 years before, during, and after the fall of the nation. His message was directed mainly toward the people of Judah, the remaining southern kingdom, after the fall of the northern kingdom of Israel.

Jeremiah was born into a family of priests and called to deliver the words of God to his people at a young age. He was a contemporary of Zephaniah, Habakkuk, Daniel, and Ezekiel. His prophetic ministry consisted of three phases: (1) pre-exile while Judah was under the threat of Assyria and Egypt, (2) Babylonian threat, siege, and destruction of Jerusalem, (3) staying in Jerusalem with survivors and then exile to Egypt. The book of Jeremiah consists of his prophecies on the judgment of Judah, the judgment of the Gentiles, and supplemental narratives of history not written by Jeremiah at the end.

Facing the judgment of God, Jeremiah encouraged his people to repent and remain faithful. His message was unpopular in his time, and he was hated and persecuted throughout his ministry. However, he delivered the message of the LORD with courage and boldness. He is known as the 'weeping prophet' not because he cried for his own pain but because he deeply cared about the people of Judah and shared the shepherd's heart of God. He deeply understood the weight of his prophecy and wept for the people and God. Even though his desperate appeal to his people was rejected and ignored, he continued guiding the people with the truth.

GOD CALLS JEREMIAH

Jeremiah 1:1-19
Key Verse 1:5

Jeremiah was born in a Levite family of priests. While he was still young (6), God called him to deliver his words to his people. The young man was reluctant to receive the calling. He felt inadequate.

However, God knew him before his birth, and he would guide him to say the right words. The message he was to bring to God's people was of punishment and destruction, yet with the hope of a future in the Lord. It was a difficult task for Jeremiah since the people had been proud and stubborn in disobeying God's will for generations. Nevertheless, God assured him not to be terrified. As God made him like a fortified city, no man will overcome him with their strength, for God will stand with him and rescue him from any men's fight (19).

Are you reluctant to answer God's calling? Do you feel weak in this world which seems too strong and stubborn? Knowing all your weaknesses, our God is calling you to participate in his work. Accept his calling and receive his vision. He will guide you where to go and what to do.

Prayer: Father, I am weak and sinful. Yet I find comfort in realizing that you know me. You know how I can be useful to you as you have formed me. Help me to have the courage to accept your calling and let you guide my life for your glory.

One Word: The Lord's calling.

TWO GREAT SINS OF JERUSALEM

Jeremiah 2:1-19
Key Verse 2:13

Jeremiah was called to deliver the message of God's judgment. The first words that came to Jeremiah showed the sin Jerusalem committed. They did not live up to keeping God's command. They abandoned God and replaced God with idols. They foolishly turned away from the streams of living water and built a cistern that could not even hold stale water (13).

In contrast, God reminds them of the early days in their history when they devoted themselves fully to God. They were disciplined in the wilderness for many years, learning to depend on God only (2,3). They did grumble, yet they always turned to God, knowing his protection and provision for them.

However, in the Promised Land, where they received all the promised blessings and comfort, they rebelled against God and turned toward worthless idols (7,8). That was the reason for the punishment they were facing. Are you looking for your salvation from anything other than our sovereign God? Remember your first love and turn to him.

Prayer: Father, you brought me out of the power of sin and death. You have been with me when I was too weak to stand alone and raised me, protecting and providing. Please be with me and help me to hold to you in times of blessing or trouble with a humble heart.

One Word: Remember God and do not turn away.

THE LORD HAS REJECTED THOSE YOU TRUST

Jeremiah 2:20-3:5
Key Verse 2:37

The people of Judah committed spiritual adultery as they turned away from God. They acted like a prostitute giving themselves to foreign gods (20). They were like unfruitful useless vines (21), stained clothes that could not be washed with soap (22), and animals in heat running after mates (23).

The people of Israel were disgraced as she tried to save herself by turning to Assyria and Egypt (26). As they turned to their gods made of stone and wood, they also thought other kings would help them out of trouble. They turned away from God's grace and ignored his punishment (30). Then what was the result? They were disappointed by Egypt and Assyria. Salvation could not be found in those places where God did not dwell (37).

By the Mosaic Law, a woman who had left her husband and married another man could not return to her first husband later (3:1). The people of Judah took God's grace for granted (4). But it was not something they could demand. They had to humbly repent and turn away from their way of evil (5).

Prayer: Father, please forgive me for my sins for turning away from you and seeking comfort elsewhere. Please accept my humble prayer as I come to you with a broken heart. I want to find comfort and peace as I live in your will.

One Word: Trust none other than the Lord.

GOD'S CALLING FOR REPENTANCE

Jeremiah 3:6-4:4
Key Verse 3:15

This is Jeremiah's prophecy during the times of King Josiah. When the people of Israel turned away from God and openly worshiped idols despite God's warning, God sent her away to captivity in Assyria (8). And Judah did not learn a lesson from Israel. They kept their appearance at the temple but did not worship God wholeheartedly.

In today's passage, God calls Israel to return and Judah to repent their unfaithful hearts. He begins his calling with a promise of hope. He is faithful and forgiving (12). He promises spiritual leaders after his own heart (15). When his name is glorified, Judah and Israel will be united and receive their inheritance again (18).

As God was glad to call them his children and be called their 'Father' (19), he also heard their cries and desired to cure them (22). God's rebuke for them also called them to acknowledge their sin and return to him. They had to circumcise their hearts to the Lord (4:4). God desires our hearts of worship (Rm 2:28-29) while he waits to pour his blessing on us (4:2).

Prayer: Father, I find my hope in your grace and forgiveness. I am blessed to come to you and call you my Father. Thank you for Jesus, my good shepherd. Please help me to be faithful to you and live in your presence.

One Word: Repent and return to God.

WARNING OF THE JUDGMENT

Jeremiah 4:5-31
Key Verse 4:19

God had given Judah numerous chances to return, but they did not listen. Now Jeremiah was to bring the message of judgment. The coming disaster would be like a scorching wind that consumes everything. No discipline they had ever received would compare to the coming judgment (11,12).

Jeremiah was in anguish delivering this message. He moaned to God for allowing them to live in their sinful pride and illusion of peace for so long (10), and his heart was pained at the vision of the coming disaster (19). Jeremiah's agony also reveals God's aching heart as he decided to bring judgment upon the people he called his own (22). While he promises there will be remnants (27), the judgment had been decided against them (28).

The people of Judah were still oblivious (10). They adorned themselves and tried to keep the peace by pleasing the powerful nations (30). As they were unwilling to listen to the prophet's desperate warning and turn back to God, they faced the judgment they could not bear (31).

Prayer: Father, you are gracious and patient with me. Help me not to take your patience for granted, remembering you are also a righteous God. Please help me to live each day faithful to you and be gracious to others as you want me to.

One Word: Judgement is a reality.

THE REASON FOR JUDGEMENT

Jeremiah 5:1-31
Key Verse 5:1

God called Jeremiah to look for one righteous person in the streets of Jerusalem. If there was one who lived by the truth, God was willing to revoke his judgment upon them (1). Jeremiah looked all over high and low. But people were stubborn and proud. The leaders deceived people by their own authority (31). They claimed to know God (2), yet did not fear God nor care about justice and mercy (22,28).

They turned away from God while they lived in the promised land, enjoying seasonal blessings (23,24). Since they served foreign gods in the land they inherited from God, they would be punished as slaves in a foreign land (19). The people of Judah saw Israel being seized by Assyrians and tried to save themselves by having a wise foreign policy with Egypt and Assyria. However, God would raise a distant nation, Babylon (15), who spoke a language unknown to them and would devour them completely. Sin deceives us into thinking we can live without God if we are wise to control our environment. Even the spiritual leaders lived in such deception (31). As a result, every single one of them was guilty and deserved judgment.

Prayer: Father, all I have is yours; your glory is my joy. Please guide me to honor you in my everyday living and glorify your name.

One Word: Stubborn hearts call for judgment.

BECAUSE THEY HAVE NOT LISTENED

Jeremiah 6:1-30
Key Verse 6:16

Verse 1 starts with 'Flee for safety.' Disaster was coming to Jerusalem, carried by people who were ready to attack at any time. The beautiful city would be given to terrible destruction. As God brought judgment upon his children, he was also warning them to flee. However, Jeremiah also knew that people with closed ears would not listen (10). They were used to the priests and prophets who spoke what they liked to hear (13-15). As one who was bringing the word of God, Jeremiah could feel the wrath of God (11).

The Lord instructed them to find a good way to walk just as their forefathers had walked with God, but they refused (16). As they repeatedly disobeyed God's will, they brought elaborate offerings that God did not care about (20). (1Sam 15:22)

God again warned them of the army coming from the north and their destruction. It was time for them to listen and sincerely repent of their sins (26). With their hearts stubborn and rebellious against God's words, they would become rejected silver, impossible to refine (29).

Prayer: Father, thank you for your gracious instructions through your word each day. Please help me to open my ears and listen so I can obey your will. Please purify my heart and take the wicked out of me.

One Word: Listen to the word of God.

JUDAH'S FALSE WORSHIP

Jeremiah 7:1-8:3
Key Verse 7:19

Jeremiah was called to deliver this message at the temple gate. The people of Judah believed Jerusalem was their fortress that could not be attacked. It was built on a hill tucked away from the coasts, and more importantly, it was the city where the temple was located (4).

However, God calls their thoughts deceptive. They thought giving burnt offerings and sacrifices accompanying elaborate service was their worship. But they forgot the essential part of God's instruction when he made them into a nation: obeying God's will (22,23). Obeying God meant honoring Him, loving their neighbors, and living an honest life (6,9, Micah 6:8).

They burned incense and gave offerings to foreign idols. They even set up idols in the house of God and practiced the despicable pagan rituals of child sacrifices in the high places (30,31). Their attitude angered God's heart. But they mainly were harming themselves (19). As they turned away from the creator God and turned to useless idols, they were disgracing themselves.

Prayer: Father, it is a privilege to come to worship and praise your name. Please help me obey you fully so I can worship you properly. Please help me to honor you and find satisfaction in my soul.

One Word: Worship God with obedience to him.

THEY LIVE IN DECEPTION

Jeremiah 8:4-9:6
Key Verse 8:9

God asks rhetorical questions to his people so they would realize the foolishness of their unrepentant hearts. They were like ones who made a wrong turn and refused to return to the right path. They clung to deceit and acted as if nothing was wrong (4-6). They wanted to think they were wise with the law of the Lord, yet they refused to live by it and ended up being more foolish than the beasts who knew the seasons and their place (7,8). As a result, they would understand that their seasons of blessings are gone only when it is too late (20).

Jeremiah was grieved to see their deceitfulness and insincerity, knowing the judgment coming their way (21,22). In chapter 9, he further expresses his distress and sorrow. He was so disappointed in them and wanted to drive them away (2), yet he shed a fountain of tears for the suffering they would go through (1). Jeremiah's shepherd's heart represents that of our Father God. As a loving Father, his heart is grieved to see his children stubbornly insist on living the way of sin and deception that would lead them to destruction. Have you stepped away from the right path? Would you get up and turn to the right path accepting the Father's word today?

Prayer: Father, thank you for giving me the desire to live by your word. Please help me not to cling to my idea and humbly accept your correction.

One Word: Come out of deception.

WHO HAS THE WISDOM TO KNOW THE LORD?

Oct. 26

Jeremiah 9:7-26
Key Verse 9:24

The people of Judah acted polished, speaking nicely to their neighbors. Yet their hearts were full of deceit, looking for a way to take advantage of others (8). They were circumcised only in the flesh, not their hearts (25,26). God, in his righteousness, could not leave them in their sin (9).

The vision of the ruins of Jerusalem brought Jeremiah to lament. The people will be scattered, and down through the generations, the women will wail over the death of their loved ones (20). Therefore, boasting about human wisdom, strength, and riches is meaningless (23). Our outward appearance does not glorify God, but we can boast of our deep relationship with God, who would lead us to kindness, justice, and righteousness (24). We can please God only when we find ourselves in him and desire to know him better. (Galatians 6:14)

Would you humbly confess your sins before God, who loved you despite your sins? Turn to our kind and gracious Father, and you will boast about his wonderful love.

Prayer: Father, I repent of my hypocrisy as I live before people instead of sincerely struggling to live by your word. Please help me to grow in my spirit to get to know you better each day.

One Word: What do I have to boast?

IDOLS ARE WORTHLESS

Jeremiah 10:1-25
Key Verse 10:16

It's natural for us to imitate the people around us and absorb their ways of thinking. But the Bible teaches us not to conform to the pattern of this world (1; Romans 12:1). This passage shows us that the business of the world is to create and worship idols. An idol is anything we strive after to satisfy our souls apart from God himself. Following idols makes us fools (8).

The people of the world make good money by creating, advertising, and selling idols, and they are very skilled at it (9). However, despite people's best efforts, they are inwardly shamed because what they produce corrupts the world and is not worthy of worship (14). God's people should choose their careers very carefully so they are not ashamed of what they produce or live for.

Idols cannot be compared to God, who created everything. He is truly worthy of worship because he is so high and holy above us (12-13). Even when we are suffering and feel that our wounds are incurable, we can put our trust in God who is our Portion (16) and who directs our life and disciplines us for our good (19, 23-24).

Prayer: Father, thank you for Jeremiah's words that warn me not to follow the idolatrous pattern of this world. Help me live only to worship you.

One Word: Creator God, not idols.

LISTEN TO THE TERMS OF THE COVENANT

Jeremiah 11:1-17
Key Verse 11:6

The Lord commanded Jeremiah to remind Israel of the terms of the covenant he made with them (1-5). God brought them out of Egypt, and he promised to make them his people if they obeyed him from then on. As God's people, their most important duty was to remember and keep that covenant. However, they broke their covenant with God, causing all of Israel's current suffering (8). They neglected to worship God and, as a result, worshiped idols like they once did in Egypt (13). This made God's judgment on them unavoidable (11).

However, God offers a new covenant with us that is greater than the one he made with Israel because it is a life-giving covenant of grace in Jesus. We enter a personal, covenant relationship with Jesus through faith in his blood. This covenant is the basis of our new life as God's people. We are naturally forgetful, and it's easy for us to live focusing only on our current situations. But if we forget God's covenant, we will fall back into sins we thought we had left behind (10). Let's read the terms of God's covenant with us in the Bible and remind each other of it also.

Prayer: Father, thank you for the covenant promise you gave me in Jesus. Help me remember your covenant and also teach it to others.

One Word: Remember God's covenant with us.

JEREMIAH STRUGGLES WITH PERSECUTION

Jeremiah 11:18-12:1-17
Key Verse 12:5

Jeremiah found out that people from the city of Anathoth were planning to kill him (11:18,21) to stop him from prophesying about God's judgment. Before God revealed the plot to him, Jeremiah was totally unaware (19), but he prayed and committed his cause to the Lord (20). Then God promised to punish those who were plotting against Jeremiah so that he would not need to take his own revenge.

Still, Jeremiah was discouraged, and he poured out his questions to God. He wondered why the wicked seemed to be successful and live at ease (12:1). What was worse, the wicked were hypocrites, speaking holy-sounding words while their hearts were far from God (2). But God reminded Jeremiah that the life of faith is like running a race (5) and that he needed perseverance to continue his mission - even when his own family members turned against him (6). Then God prophesied his judgment again through Jeremiah, but this time, God also promised his redemption (15).

When we grow weary of standing against all the evil in the world and we don't know who is on God's side, we can take assurance in God's protection and hear his challenge to keep running.

Prayer: Father, help me to not be fearful of what people can do, but to keep doing the work you gave me with a pure heart. Give me strength to keep running the race of faith.

One Word: Keep running the race.

A LINEN BELT

Jeremiah 13:1-27
Key Verse 13:11

When the Lord had Jeremiah hide a linen belt in a crevice in the rocks, and then take it out later to find it rotted, it was to show how sin ruins our lives. God wanted the people of Israel to be bound to him in love like a belt for his renown and praise and honor (11). Linen garments were worn by Israel's priests and represented holiness (Lev 16:32). But Israel refused to pay attention to his word and kept worshiping idols. Now they were defiled and unable to reveal God's glory like Jeremiah's useless belt.

We also were created to reveal God's glory, but we became so accustomed to sinning and doing evil that we were unable to do good (23). Our sinful actions, which can be compared to adultery against God, corrupted our hearts (27) until we were like the useless belt. We deserve God's judgment, like Israel was (22). But thank God that he had mercy on us in our useless condition and sent his Son. Jesus' blood cleanses us from the filth of sin and makes us holy. It is like Jesus clothes us newly in fine linen (Rev 19:7-8), so we can bring God praise and honor with our lives.

Prayer: Father, thank you for Jesus. Help me remember how sin made me useless. Keep me bound to you in Jesus for your glory.

One Word: *Bound to Jesus for his glory.*

THE WEEPING PROPHET

Jeremiah 14:1-22
Key Verse 14:17

Judah was suffering from a severe drought that was the consequence of their sins. Jeremiah prayed, confessing that his people had often rebelled, but he asked the Lord not to forsake the people who bore his name (9). Some so-called prophets were proclaiming that Judah would not suffer, but they were prophesying falsely. They were just saying what people wanted to hear (14).

The Lord told Jeremiah not to pray for the people because he had decided to punish them (11-12). But this was really just a test of Jeremiah's heart. Jeremiah was determined to keep praying for his people with tears, night and day without ceasing, if by any means they could be spiritually healed (17). Sometimes, God's people need a "weeping prophet", as Jeremiah is called. When we see the evil and suffering in our times, we can be tempted to give up on the people of the world. But God is the source of undying hope. We should pray to God for the world no matter what, even if his judgment seems inescapable.

Prayer: Father, I confess that we are a sinful people who wander from you so much. But I believe you put me here to be an intercessor. May the tearful prayers of your saints work for good in the world.

One Word: Pray for the sinful world with tears.

JEREMIAH'S PAIN

Jeremiah 15:1-21
Key Verse 15:19

The Lord was going to bring about the complete destruction of Judah and Jerusalem (1-3). He prophesied this through Jeremiah, so Israel would know that it was the result of their great sin. With each generation, Judah slid further and further from God, culminating in the evil king Manasseh, who practiced every kind of cruelty and idolatry over a 55-year reign (4). This should remind us that once we begin to slide away from God, it is very difficult to change our direction.

The message that Jeremiah had to bring was almost too much for him to bear. Though he had never taken advantage of anyone, everyone cursed him because he brought words of judgment (10). The Lord tried to comfort Jeremiah (11), but still, Jeremiah asks: Why do I have to suffer so much pain when I only deny myself to serve you? (18) In reply, the Lord commands Jeremiah to repent and recommit himself to speak only worthy words, not becoming like people of the world (19).

It is indeed too hard for us to keep standing against the pattern of the world with our own strength. But if we commit ourselves to God and resolve to speak only his words, no one will be able to overcome us (20-21).

Prayer: Father, thank you for the privilege of being your messenger, even when it brings trouble. Let my true joy be in your words.

One Word: Speak worthy words.

November

Sun	Mon	Tue	Wed	Thu	Fri	Sat
			1	2	3	4
5	6	7	8	9	10	11
12	13	14	15	16	17	18
19	20	21	22	23	24	25
26	27	28	29	30		

THE INHERITANCE OF JUDAH

Joshua 15:1-63
Key Verse 15:1

The land of Canaan was distributed among the twelve tribes of Israel. Through Caleb's faith (Num 13), the tribe of Judah was recognized as the prominent tribe, but that came with big responsibilities. First, they needed to fight and take possession of the allotted land from the Canaanites and set an example for the other tribes. Second, they needed to provide security to the other tribes from Israel's southern enemies: the Egyptians, the Philistines and the Edomites. God-pleasing-faith brings great blessings as well as responsibility to help and protect His people.

Caleb received a portion of the land of Judah as his inheritance, but first needed to drive out the Anakites. Caleb drove them out with God's help and then pressed on to the city of Debir. He offered his daughter Acsah in marriage to the man who would capture it with faith and courage. Othniel stepped forward, delivered Debir and took Acsah as his wife, but Judah could not drive out the Jebusites in Jerusalem. God promised the land, but they needed to claim it by an act of faith. God's promises are given to those who claim them by faith.

Prayer: Lord, help me to walk in obedience and faith to your word and cling to your promises.

One Word: Faith in action.

GO, CLEAR LAND FOR YOURSELVES

Joshua 16:1-17:18
Key Verse 17:15

The tribes of Ephraim and Manasseh, the sons of Joseph, received their allotted land. Then from the tribe of Manasseh, the five daughters of Zelophehad, who had no son, came to Joshua and claimed the land that Moses had promised to give them (Nu 27). They had petitioned both to Moses and to Joshua challenging the firm norms by their faith and courage. God honored these women's faith and courage and gave them an inheritance.

The tribes Ephraim and Manasseh complained that the land was not enough for them, because they neither cleared the forest nor drove out the powerful Canaanites equipped with iron chariots. Joshua saw that their real problem was not lack of land, but lack of faith, vision and fighting spirit. So, he encouraged them to be strong in the Lord to clear the forest to its farthest limits and drive their enemies out. Without faith, we see only obstacles and formidable enemies and complain. By faith we can see "spacious land" and great blessing beyond obstacles and enemies. Faith causes us to quit complaining and hold to what God has promised.

Prayer: Lord, help me to have faith and courage so that I may see God's great promises and hold onto them boldly. Help me to clear the land.

One Word: Go up and clear land for yourselves.

DIVIDING THE LAND

Joshua 18:1-19:51
Key Verse 18:3

After seven years of war, the land of Canaan was subdued, and the tabernacle was finally set up. But seven of the tribes were not interested in their inheritance since it would involve more warfare and struggle. They wanted to retire and relax. Joshua knew their fatigue, so he held a conference at Shiloh to renew their spirit and strength before God to complete their conquest. Complacency in the Christian life is usually the mark of weariness or a distant relationship with God. "Those who hope in the Lord will renew their strength. They will soar on wings like eagles…" (Is 40:31).

Three men from each tribe went out to survey the land. Perhaps Joshua wanted them to see first-hand how good the land was, and to have the desire to take it. By taking possession of the land between Judah on the south and Joseph on the north, they could gain the final victory and fulfill God's promise. The surveyors went out and recorded all the details. Then Joshua cast lots and made assignments for the seven tribes. Our priceless inheritance is kept in heaven. And we are to push on through the struggles to receive it.

Prayer: Lord, I come to renew my relationship with you. Give me strength to continue serving your mission.

One Word: How long will you wait?

CITIES OF REFUGE

Joshua 20:1-9
Key Verse 20:2

God had spoken to Moses about cities of refuge in Exodus 21. These cities were to be an integral part of their justice system. A manslayer who accidentally killed a person could flee to these cities to be protected against the avenger of blood. The six cities of refuge were designated throughout the land. These cities were God's appointed places, where the slayer would receive protection, justice and mercy. God cares for all people without partiality and maintains His perfect mercy and justice. Jesus is the ultimate God-appointed city of refuge. Anyone who comes to Him in faith will receive His mercy, justice, and protection.

The slayer who was proven innocent had to dwell in the city of refuge until the death of the high priest. Although the slayer would be granted pardon, the loss of life was still considered a very serious matter. The death of the priest in a way was considered a substitute for the slayer. The slayer would be acquitted of his transgression and would be able to go back home. This points us ultimately to the death of Jesus, our great high priest who paid for all our sins.

Prayer: Lord, thank you for Jesus, the city of refuge for all sinners including sinners like me.

One Word: Jesus is the city of refuge.

NOT ONE OF GOD'S PROMISES FAILED

Joshua 21:1-45
Key Verse 21:45

According to God's command, the Levites received no inheritance of the land. Rather, they were given several towns and pasturelands from among the inheritances of the other tribes. The Levites were scattered throughout the land of Israel. This way each tribe would have a priestly influence and presence among them. Priests were chosen not to be served but to serve God and His people. As "a royal priesthood" (1 Pe 2:9), Christians are to be scattered throughout the world and become salt and light. They are called to serve people around them.

God fulfilled His promised to give the land to Israel. All the tribes took possession of the land and settled there. God also gave them rest from war and rest from their enemies as He had promised their forefathers. God's promises to their forefathers turned into a reality. God is faithful in keeping his promises even though we often fail to keep our promises to Him. All of God's promises are "good," (45) because God is good. God's good promises never fail and lead us to rest.

Prayer: Lord, thank you for your "good" promises. Help me to hold onto them and pass them on to the next generation.

One Word: God's promises are good.

THE EASTERN TRIBES RETURN HOME

Joshua 22:1-9
Key Verse 22:5

The conquest of Canaan had ended, and the land was divided into twelve tribes. Then Joshua dismissed the two and a half tribes of those in the Transjordan with honor. They had kept their promise to Moses and helped the other tribes in the conquest faithfully. As he sent them to their families, Joshua reminded them to remain faithful to the Lord—loving Him, walking in obedience to Him, keeping His commands, holding fast to Him, and serving him. God's people need to be both encouraged and challenged to remain faithful to the Lord in their lives of faith. We are not to rest on our laurels but keep on living by faith (Phil 3:13-14). *an emblem of prosperity & fame*

Joshua didn't send them away empty handed but gave them blessing and bounty. They received the fruit of faithful living. Obedience to God and faithfulness to Christ bring God's great blessings. Jesus says, "But seek first his kingdom and his righteousness, and all these things will be given to you as well" (Mt 6:33).

Prayer: Lord, thank you for giving me a mission to spread the gospel. Help me to complete it. Remind me of living by faith to the end.

One Word: Keep on running the race of faith.

A MISUNDERSTANDING CLEARED UP

Joshua 22:10-34
Key Verse 22:31

As the eastern tribes crossed the Jordan to return to their homes, they built an altar by the Jordan. They were determined to be faithful to God and set up an altar to testify of God's faithfulness and their covenant commitment to Him. It would also remind them that they were to identify with the 12 tribes and express their unity with the Western tribes. However, the Western tribes misunderstood this as idolatrous worship and were ready to go to war. The Eastern tribes patiently explained their case and motives and avoided an all out conflict. It is important to note that both sides were zealous for the glory of God. After receiving clarity in the situation, they rejoiced and blessed God together.

Christians are to keep both the purity and unity of the church. Sometimes, however, we refuse to listen to one another and fail to keep unity. Regrettably we may tolerate sin and draw back from controversy to keep unity and peace. In His high priestly prayer, Jesus prayed for His people to be sanctified by the truth (Jn 17:17), and to be brought to complete unity (Jn 17:23). Jesus' people are to zealously pursue the purity and unity of the church.

Prayer: Lord, help us grow in Jesus so that we may build up your church with purity as well as unity.

One Word: Unity in purity.

LOVE THE LORD YOUR GOD

Joshua 23:1-16
Key Verse 23:11

What would your parting words be to the Christian leaders in our nation? If you followed Joshua's example, you would remind them of all the magnificent things God has done and of all the wonderful things he has promised. Joshua reminded the leaders of Israel that it was God who fought for them and gave them victory over all the nations they had conquered. It was God who allotted an inheritance to each of the tribes of Israel. Now, their task was to claim this inheritance by driving out the nations that remained by faith. God promised to push the remaining nations back and to drive them out of their sight so his people could possess the land. They were to cling to God by obeying his word and loving him instead of mingling with the other nations and adopting their gods. Failure to do so would result in these nations being a trap and a snare to them and their land being forfeited.

God kept all the promises he had made to his people. Without exception, God fulfills each and every one of his promises. God promised good things for his people if they kept his covenant, and evil things if they broke it. If they served other gods and bowed down to them, God promised that they would perish quickly from the land. The choice was theirs. What would the leaders decide?

Prayer: Father, help us to obey your word.

One Word: Be very careful to love God.

THE WONDERFUL GIFT OF GOD

Joshua 24:1-13
Key Verse 24:13

Joshua gathered all the leaders and tribes of Israel at Shechem. It was time for the nation to reflect on all the things God had done and how they should live as his people. In verse 13, God reminds his people that he had given them a land that they had not labored for, cities that they had not built, and luscious vineyards and orchards that they did not plant. Indeed, they were enjoying the abundant blessings of God. How did they get to this place? It was God's grace every step of the way! Abraham and his father were idolaters when God called Abraham and established his covenant with him. It was God who fulfilled his promises and blessed Abraham with a whole nation of descendants. God delivered his people from Egypt, provided for them in the wilderness, and fought for them in the land of Canaan. It was all the one-sided grace of God.

Like the Israelites, it is good for Christians to pause and reflect on the wonderful grace of God in their lives. In Christ, we have received a new birth into a living hope and an inheritance that will never perish, spoil, or fade. We have been seated in the heavenly realms with Christ and have been adopted as children of God. One day, we will be with Christ forever. We will see him in all his glory and we will be like him. How is this possible? It is the work and gift of our amazing God.

Prayer: Father, we honor and praise you.

One Word: Salvation is the gift of our God.

CHOOSE WHOM YOU WILL SERVE

Joshua 24:14-28
Key Verses 24:14

How would the people of Israel respond to the grace of God? How would their lives be changed? By accepting God's gift of salvation, we commit ourselves to living as his holy and redeemed people. Joshua says, "Now therefore fear the LORD and serve him in sincerity and in faithfulness." We put aside the false gods of this world and worship the true and living God. We serve him in sincerity with all our hearts by making his honor and glory our one passion and desire. We serve him in faithfulness by obeying his word as the absolute authority in our lives. He is our God and we are his people. Serving him is the choice that we make each and every day.

The people of Israel confessed everything the LORD had done for them and promised to serve him as their God. However, in verse 19, Joshua says, "You are not able to serve the LORD, for he is a holy God." They should have realized that they were not able to serve God with their own strength. Salvation is by the power of God and so is sanctification. We need God's help to obey his commands and live lives that honor him. We must be fully surrendered and dependent on Him. Joshua set up a large stone by the sanctuary of the LORD as a witness to the commitment they made. Then, every man went to his inheritance.

Prayer: Father, give us strength to serve you.

One Word: Choose the LORD your God!

GIVE BACK TO GOD WHAT IS GOD'S

Luke 20:19-26
Key Verse 20: 25

The religious leaders were offended by Jesus' warning through the parable, but they couldn't arrest him right away because they were afraid of the people. They sent spies to trap him into doing or saying something that would get him in trouble with the Roman government. "Is it right for us to pay taxes to Caesar or not?" If Jesus said yes, he would appear to support evil to the eyes of people. If Jesus said no, then he was inciting a riot against Rome. Jesus let them show him a denarius and asked them, "Whose image and inscription are on it?" They replied, "Caesars." Then, Jesus said, "Then give back to Caesar what is Caesar's and to God what is God's."

Like the tenants in the parable, they did not want to give their due to anyone, either to the governing authority or to God. But Jesus said to them to give their due both to Rome and to God. As Caesar's image and inscription were on a Roman coin, so we have God's image in us. We have a basic duty toward God and to our country. However, duty to God supersedes duty to our country. Since God's people have a dual citizenship, they should not evade their duty to God, their Creator. We owe everything to God and must give him our love, obedience, and worship.

Prayer: Lord, help me love and worship you and live for your glory in my daily life while fulfilling my basic duty to my country.

One Word: Give to God; give to Caesar.

GOD OF THE LIVING

Luke 20:27-44
Key Verse 20:38

The Sadducees did not believe in <u>life after death;</u> they were religious leaders, but practical atheists. They came to Jesus with a hypothetical, but unrealistic question (28-33). They intended to make Jesus' teaching about the resurrection look absurd, but they only revealed their spiritual ignorance and godless way of thinking. They wanted to live forever on earth, enjoying their wealth and power. In reality, they lived in despair under the power of death, for they didn't have faith in the resurrection. But there is resurrection from the dead and those who participate in the resurrection can no longer die for they will be clothed with a glorious resurrection body fit for heaven like that of the Risen Christ. The children of God will enjoy eternal life in heaven. Heaven is not an extension of life on earth.

God is the God of the living. Anyone who believes in God will not end in death, but they will be made alive in Christ. Those who are blinded from seeing God in Jesus may be alive physically, but spiritually are dead. Those who have faith and walk in the footsteps of Abraham, Isaac, and Jacob are the living. They will be victors over the power of sin and death in Jesus, David's Lord, and will reign with Christ in the kingdom.

Prayer: Lord, thank you for the glorious hope of resurrection in Christ. Open my spiritual eyes to see the God of the living and live with resurrection faith in my daily life.

One Word: Hope in the God of the living.

THE WIDOW'S OFFERING

Luke 20:45-21:4
Key Verse 21:4

The teachers of the law looked pious, but they were hypocritical. They went to the marketplaces to show off their fancy robes and to be greeted by people; they wanted to be treated as VIPs at banquets or in the synagogues. They did not seek God and his glory; rather they used God's name to seek human glory and people's recognition. They used religion as a cloak for taking advantage of weak people for their material gain. Jesus said that this kind of people will be punished most severely. Jesus wants us to live in the sight of God, seeking God's glory.

As Jesus was standing in the temple, he saw some rich people putting a large amount of money into the treasury of the temple out of their wealth. But a poor widow put in two very small copper coins, which were the smallest unit of coinage in Jewish currency and were of very little value. But she put in all she had to live on out of poverty. It was worth more than money. She did not calculate or offer leftovers, but gave everything she had, proportionally more than the rich. Jesus saw her sacrificial heart and faith. In Jesus' eyes, her gift was the most expensive of all, for she gave God her heart and trusted him for her future. This was her faith.

Prayer: Lord, help me to seek you and your glory and give cheerfully for those who are in need out of love. Grant me eyes to see beautiful acts of love and faith in others.

One Word: Jesus valued a widow's gift to God.

STAND FIRM

Luke 21:5-19
Key Verse 21:19

The destruction of the temple sounded like the end of the world to Jesus' disciples. They asked Jesus, "When?" and "What signs?" Jesus' answer tells us how to live in a world tainted by evil and rebellion, idolatry, and immorality. Jesus warns us of deception of the anti-Christs and false prophets who try to lead God's people astray. We need to know Jesus personally and have a sound understanding of the Bible not to be misled by all kinds of false teachings and ideas. There will be all kinds of natural and human-caused disasters such as wars, earthquakes, famines which frighten us. But we must not be fearful, for God is in control and is working out his purpose even in the midst of these things.

We may be persecuted, betrayed, and hated by the world or even close ones on account of Jesus' name. It is not easy for anyone to bear it. However, we shouldn't worry or become fearful, for Jesus promises to give us his word and wisdom. It can be an opportunity for us to witness to Jesus. If we don't compromise, but stand firm on Jesus' side, we will gain life.

Prayer: Lord, help me not to be deceived, but to witness to Jesus and to stand firm.

One Word: Stand firm on God's side.

THE SON OF MAN COMING IN A CLOUD

Luke 21:20-28
Key Verse: 21:27

Jesus' prediction of the destruction of Jerusalem came true in 70 A.D. by Titus, a Roman general. It was the time of distress and wrath against the people of Israel. Many people were killed by the sword and taken as prisoners. It was God's punishment on his people who rejected Jesus, the Messiah, who came to save them. Jerusalem would be trampled on until the times of the Gentiles have been fulfilled (20:16; Ro 11:25).

The destruction of Jerusalem is a foreshadow of the final judgment when Jesus comes again to judge the world and restore all things. Before his coming, there will be ominous signs in the earth and sky which will bring anguish and perplexity. The Lord Jesus will come in power and great glory as the King of kings and Lord of lords. It will be a day of terror for those who rejected him, but it will be a glorious day of rejoicing and victory for those who belong to him. Jesus' people don't need to be fearful of the signs of the end of the age but must stand firm and lift up their heads to welcome their coming Redeemer and King. When he comes again, a new heaven and earth will come, and we will live in his presence and reign with him forever. This is our living hope in Christ.

Prayer: Lord, thank you for the glorious promise of the second coming of Jesus. Help me to live by faith while waiting for this second coming.

One Word: Jesus is coming again with power and great glory!

BE ALWAYS ON THE WATCH AND PRAY

Luke 21:29-38
Key Verse 21:36

Jesus does not want us to see the world negatively and despair at what is happening but have prophetic insight to see the world from God's point of view, for the kingdom of God is near. As Jesus promised, he will surely come, though we don't know when. So, we must be careful not to let our hearts be weighed down by the anxiety of life and fleeting pleasures of the world, for the day will come suddenly like a trap. Jesus wants us to be spiritually alert and ready for his second coming.

It is easy to take Jesus' warning lightly and become complacent. Jesus says, "Be always on the watch and pray" so that we may be counted worthy to escape God's judgment and stand before Jesus. Jesus spent his last days by teaching the word at the temple every day and spent the night at the Mount of Olives. People came to the temple early in the morning to hear the word of God from Jesus. Learning the word of God like the people and teaching the word of God like Jesus can be an effective way to watch and pray as we wait for the second coming of our Lord Jesus Christ. Learning and teaching the word of God enables us to stand before Jesus by overcoming the world.

Prayer: Lord, grant us spiritual insight to see the world from God's point of view and enable us to watch and pray, waiting for our Lord's second coming.

One Word: Watch and pray!

THE NEW COVENANT IN JESUS' BLOOD

Luke 22:1-23
Key Verse 22:20

As the Passover was approaching, the religious leaders were looking for some way to get rid of Jesus. Judas was one of the Twelve, but he became a betrayer of his master for money. Luke says that Satan entered him. That's what happened when Judas didn't accept Jesus' love and word to the end. Now he watched for an opportunity to hand Jesus over to the enemies.

Jesus sent Peter and John to go into the city to prepare the Passover. It would be the Last Supper with his disciples before his arrest. Jesus wanted to teach them the meaning of his death and plant hope in the kingdom of God. During the Passover meal Jesus broke the bread and gave it to his disciples saying, "This is my body given for you; do this in remembrance of me." Then he gave them the cup, saying, "This cup is the new covenant in my blood, which is poured out for you." The bread and the cup represent Jesus' broken body and his shed blood on the cross. God's promise to forgive our sins was sealed by Jesus' death on the cross. If we repent and accept Jesus' atoning death for us, we freely receive the forgiveness of our sins and become family members of God; we are reconciled to God and can serve the living God. This new covenant sealed by Jesus' blood is for anyone who believes in Jesus.

Prayer: Lord, help me remember your grace of forgiveness and live as your covenant people.

One Word: Jesus shed his blood for my sins.

I CONFER ON YOU A KINGDOM

Luke 22:24-38
Key Verse 22:29

Those who exercise authority and power over others are considered great in the world. The disciples envied worldly rulers and wanted to be like them. However, Jesus told them that truly great people are those who serve others. Jesus is the Son of God, but he used his power to serve the weak, sick, and helpless in his life and ministry. Jesus encouraged his disciples to learn how to serve others by following his example. Jesus' people do not follow the way of the world, but choose to follow the footsteps of Jesus, for their hope is not in this world, but in the eternal kingdom of God.

Jesus knew that Satan would shake Peter's faith when he was arrested. Jesus also knew that Peter would fail to keep his faith. However, Jesus still prayed for Peter that his faith might not fail and that he might strengthen his brothers after turning back from failure. Jesus knows our weakness, but he is praying for us not to fail in our faith. When we fail, we must never despair, but come to God in repentance and receive his forgiveness. Christians are called to engage in a spiritual battle with Satan and to bring the gospel to the ends of the earth. For this, we must depend on God alone, not on material things or people or past experiences.

Prayer: Lord, help me put my hope in your kingdom and live a life of service. Help me not to fail in faith.

One Word: Jesus confers on us a kingdom.

NOT MY WILL, BUT YOURS BE DONE

Luke 22:39-53
Key Verse 22:42

After the Last Supper, Jesus went out as usual to the Mount of Olives to pray. There, he knelt and prayed, "Father, if you are willing, take this cup from me; yet not my will, but yours be done" (42). Jesus knew his Father's will for him: it was to die on the cross as the Lamb of God, bearing God's wrath on his body and being forsaken. Jesus wanted to avoid it. He fought a fierce spiritual battle through prayer to submit to the will of his Father until he could say, "not my will, but yours be done." His prayer was so earnest that his sweat was like drops of blood falling to the ground. God strengthened him through an angel. Now he was ready to face the cross; but the disciples were not, for they did not prepare through prayer.

An armed crowd led by Judas came to arrest Jesus. Judas approached Jesus like a friend and kissed him, hiding his evil intention. Jesus gave him the last opportunity to repent, saying, "Judas, are you betraying the Son of Man with a kiss?" It was a kiss of betrayal. When Jesus was arrested, his followers wanted to fight with swords by striking the ear of the high priest's servant. However, Jesus stopped them, for it was not his way. He even healed the servant. Jesus' way was not the way of swords, but the way of obedience and submission to the will of God even when darkness reigned.

Prayer: Father, help me to pray like Jesus until I may submit to your will for me and follow your way.

One Word: Not my will, but yours be done!

THE SON OF MAN WILL BE SEATED AT THE RIGHT HAND OF THE MIGHTY GOD

Luke 22:54-71
Key Verse 22:69

Jesus was led to the high priest to be tried. Peter was loyal to Jesus, but he was not prepared for the crisis, for he did not pray like Jesus. So, he followed at a distance without a decision of faith. Then he sat down around the fire, pretending to be one of them. However, when confronted by a servant girl, he denied even knowing Jesus out of fear. After the first denial, the next two came easily. Just then, the rooster crowed and Jesus turned and looked straight at him. Peter went out and wept bitterly.

Jesus silently bore the soldiers' mockery, beating, and insult like a lamb led to the slaughter (Isa 53:7). However, Jesus was not silent before the council. When they asked Jesus if he was the Messiah, he claimed to be the Messiah (68). When they asked him if he was the Son of God, he said, "I am" (70), not hiding his identity, though he knew that his answer would cause his death. At this, they condemned Jesus as guilty of blasphemy. Jesus was tried before the council as a criminal, though innocent, but he was confident of his victory, having a resurrection faith that he would sit on the throne of God as the Sovereign Ruler and Judge over all mankind through his death and resurrection.

Prayer: Lord, help me to repent like Peter when I fail and live with unshakable faith in your kingdom.

One Word: Sinless Jesus was tried in my place.

JESUS WAS TRIED AND CONDEMNED FOR ME

Luke 23:1-25
Key Verse 23:25

The Jewish leaders handed over Jesus to Pilate, the Roman governor and pressed three charges against him: sedition, opposing paying taxes, and claiming be a king. After interrogating him, Pilate found no basis for a charge against Jesus. Knowing that Jesus was from Galilee, he sent him to Herod. Herod tried to make Jesus entertain him. Finally, to ridicule and mock Jesus and the Jews, he dressed Jesus in an elegant robe and sent him back to Pilate. Both Herod and Pilate knew Jesus had done nothing to deserve death and didn't want to be responsible for condemning Jesus.

Pilate should have set Jesus free, for Jesus was found innocent. But to appease the religious leaders, he wanted to punish Jesus and then release him. But his plan of compromise did not work, for the mob, incited by the chief priests, shouted, "Crucify him!" Pilate tried to release Jesus several times, but the crowd shouted until their shouts prevailed. Pilate was a coward and a pragmatist because he knew the truth but failed to stand on the side of the truth to secure his benefits. Jesus was tried unfairly and judged unjustly. Jesus, the innocent, was condemned in the place of the guilty including me.

Prayer: Lord, I am the one who should be tried and condemned in the court of the righteous God due to my sins. But you were tried and condemned in my place. Thank you, Jesus.

One Word: In my place, Jesus was condemned.

TODAY YOU WILL BE WITH ME IN PARADISE

Luke 23:26-43
Key Verse 23:34

As Jesus was led to the place of execution, he fell again and again under the weight of the cross. The soldiers seized Simon from Cyrene and made him carry it behind Jesus. Following Jesus, many women mourned and wailed for him. Jesus told them not to weep for him, but for them and their children, because of the judgment to come on their nation which rejected the Messiah. In light of God's righteous judgment, everyone must weep for their sins and ask for God's mercy before it is too late.

Reaching Calvary, they crucified Jesus along with two criminals (Isa 53:12). In his unbearable pain and agony on the cross, Jesus prayed to his Father God for the forgiveness of those who were killing him in their ignorance. This forgiveness is available to anyone who comes to him in repentance and faith. The soldiers cast lots to divide Jesus' clothes and mocked him along with the onlookers and rulers: "Save yourself." But they did not know that in order to save all sinners, Jesus could not save himself. One criminal admitted that he was guilty and his punishment was just and asked Jesus' mercy on him, "Jesus, remember me when you come into your kingdom." Jesus accepted him as he was and invited him to the kingdom of God.

Prayer: Lord, thank you for forgiving my sins. Help me to live as a forgiven sinner with my hope in your kingdom.

One Word: Jesus forgives and welcomes repentant sinners.

SHOUT FOR JOY

Psalm 100:1-5
Key Verse 100:3

I believe that God created us because he imagined that we would like it. However, not every day is a joyous occasion. While some look forward to spending sweet time with family, others may be lonely or be grieving a loss. While it may not always feel like it, all life is a gift from God. Every day we inhabit this life, we can experience all its wonders and emotions. In our joy, it is OK and good to shout, sing, and dance. If we are sad, it is OK to cry out. One woman I know shouted "Praise the Lord!" both at her son's wedding and at her husband's funeral. It was a beautiful testimony to God's love and mercy in all things.

God is our creator, and he is good. In love, he created us and gave us life. In love, he sustains us. In love, he provides when we humbly ask him. When we live in humility and gratitude, each day may be filled with joy, grace, and hope.

Prayer: Lord, thank you for your love and life-giving spirit poured out on us.

One Word: His love endures forever.

JESUS DIED AND WAS BURIED

Luke 23:44-56
Key Verse 23:46

While Jesus was hanging on the cross, darkness came over the whole land from noon to 3 p.m. Even the sun seemed to turn its face from the injustice of sinful humanity. Jesus breathed his last with a loud cry, committing his spirit to his loving Father. His death was not a defeat or tragedy, but a glorious victory over sin and death, a victory of God's love over Satan's hatred. The curtain of the temple blocked sinful men to come to the presence of the holy God. Now that curtain was torn in two. Jesus' shed blood opened 'a new and living way' for all sinners to go to God, be forgiven and have peace with God. Seeing what had happened, even the centurion, a hardened Gentile, praised God and testified, "Surely this was a righteous man." Those women loyal to Jesus stood at a distance, watching all these things.

Joseph, a member of the council, courageously went to Pilate to ask for Jesus' body. It was an act of courageous faith. In this way he identified himself as a follower of Jesus. He took down Jesus' body from the cross, wrapped it in linen cloth and placed in a new tomb cut in the rock. Jesus was buried and now the stage was set for his glorious resurrection.

Prayer: Lord, thank you for opening the way into the presence of God for me and all sinners. Help me live and die victoriously like Jesus..

One Word: A new and living way to God.

HE IS NOT HERE; HE HAS RISEN!

Luke 24:1-12
Key Verse 24:5b-6

On the first day of the week, very early in the morning, several women went to the tomb of Jesus with spices to embalm his dead body as their last tribute to Jesus. But they found the stone rolled away from the tomb and his body gone. Suddenly two angels stood beside them and told the good news, "Why do you look for the living among the dead? He is not here; he has risen!" As he had promised, Jesus has risen from the dead and is alive here and now (7). When they remembered Jesus' words through the angels' message, they were convinced that Jesus had risen! They felt inexpressible joy and hope and ran to tell the good news to the apostles.

The Eleven apostles were still in a state of shock because of the tragic death of their Master. They were moaning with sorrow, trembling with fear, and sitting in despair caused by their shattered dreams of the earthly messianic kingdom. So, the women's message of good news of the resurrection of Jesus seemed like nonsense. Peter ran to the tomb to see for himself. He saw the empty tomb and realized that something had happened. But he was only bewildered by what he had seen. He needed to meet the Risen Christ like those women.

Prayer: Lord, you are my Risen Lord and Saviour. Empower me with your resurrection power to live as a witness of your resurrection throughout my life.

One Word: Jesus has risen! He is alive!

JESUS EXPLAINED THE SCRIPTURES

Luke 24:13-35
Key Verse 24:27

Two disciples were on the road to Emmaus, talking and discussing everything about Jesus' life and death. Along the way Jesus joined them, but they couldn't recognize him. As Jesus joined their conversation, they talked about Jesus' powerful words and deeds, how they put their hope in him to redeem Israel, how the religious leaders handed him over to be crucified, and about the empty tomb as well as the women's testimony about the angels' message. Then Jesus rebuked their slowness to believe what the prophets had written in light of all that had happened. Jesus began to teach them the Bible all over again beginning with Moses and all the Prophets, explaining what was said in the Scriptures concerning himself. But still, they didn't recognize him because of unbelief and despair in their hearts.

When they were at the table later, Jesus took bread, gave thanks, broke it and gave it to them. Then their eyes were opened and recognized the Risen Christ. They returned at once to Jerusalem. It was not the time for them to go back to their old lives, but to share with others the good news of the kingdom of God through Jesus' death and resurrection.

Prayer: Lord, open my heart to your word and reveal yourself to me until my heart is burning with your love and share it with others.

One Word: Open my heart to see Christ.

IN HIS NAME TO ALL NATIONS

Luke 24:36-53
Key Verse 24:47

The Risen Jesus visited the apostles and conferred on them real peace. But they were frightened and thought they saw a ghost. Jesus showed his nail-pierced hands and feet then let them touch him. When they still couldn't believe because of joy and amazement, Jesus ate a piece of broiled fish before them. Jesus gave them many convincing proofs to plant in them resurrection faith. Jesus labored to help them to have resurrection faith so that they may live as witnesses of his resurrection. The gospel of Jesus' death and resurrection is the fulfillment of God's promises in the Old Testament. God wants to save all his children through the gospel of Jesus. The good news must be spread to all nations. Jesus wanted his disciples to be his witnesses in the whole world so that repentance for the forgiveness of sins would be preached in his name to the ends of the earth. He promised to send the Holy Spirit to empower them but they had to stay in Jerusalem and wait.

After giving them the world mission command, he was taken up into heaven. They worshiped him and returned to Jerusalem with great joy.

Prayer: Lord, you died and rose again and became my Lord and Savior. Help me live as your witness and share the good news of my Lord Jesus Christ.

One Word: The forgiveness of sins in His name.

LOVE COVERS OVER ALL WRONGS

Proverbs 10:1-18
Key Verse 10:12

Jesus is wisdom in the flesh. One of the most, if not *the* most, notable attributes of Jesus and God is love. Jesus did not come to judge but to love and forgive a sinful and lost humanity. Jesus sought out the outcasts and sinners including tax collectors and prostitutes. In love, he turned their failures into fertile soil where God's love took root and blossomed into new and beautiful life.

Having wisdom is not about being superior to others, but it is growing to love and embrace all people, including those who are deemed wicked. In love, we reconcile with others and help others be reconciled to God. We should not create legalistic divisions but have mercy and compassion on others. Doing this is not easy, but nothing meaningful comes easy. We should not be lazy to work towards loving others enough that covers over all their wrongs. We can do this by knowing God's love for us.

Prayer: Lord, your greatest wisdom is love that covers, forgives, and heals all our wrongs. May we also do so to others.

One Word: Love one another.

JOY

Proverbs 10:19-32
Key Verse 10:28

There are many "blessings" that we seek out in the world. It's easy for us to think: If only we have enough money, are healthy enough, beautiful enough, or holy enough, we will be satisfied. But these are never enough and end up amounting to disappointment in the end. Beauty fades, the body weakens, our holier than thou theology makes us self-righteous and divisive, and money can only go so far.

"The prospect of the righteous is joy." Joy is deeper than fleeting pleasures. Jesus' coming was heralded as good news of great joy to all people (Lk 2:10). In the Bible, joy is often expressed in relation to what one receives from God and also in relation to others' well-being. There is joy when we realize that God's love is greater than all our sins and shortcomings. God has come to help us in our sufferings and failures. He gives us new life and hope. God's joy is when one lost child is found, and we share his joy when we care for and help others in their need. Joy is multiplied when shared with others.

Prayer: Lord, give us the joy of your salvation. You came to love us in our lost-ness. May our joy increase as we share in your love for others.

One Word: Be joyful.

HUMILITY

Proverbs 11:1-15
Key Verse 11:2

Wisdom is vast and varied. We may be wise about one thing but fail miserably at others. Pride is universal and is present in even the brightest of people. Although King Solomon brought great prosperity and peace during his lifetime, he left the kingdom of Israel in great disarray after his death (1 Kings 11). On the other hand, Jesus did not seek power and glory in his time on earth. Instead, he died on the cross and became the resurrected Lord of God's kingdom which has endured and expanded beyond the rise and fall of many empires. Jesus is God who came to earth born as a helpless baby in a manger. He came to love the most needy and wretched people, approachable and welcoming to all.

Pride and arrogance have been the downfall of many powerful people and have hurt many more in their pathway. A little humility goes a long way in creating a community of love and respect that endures for many generations. It takes humility to love and accept all kinds of people, to repent and ask for help, and to recover from failures with dignity and new hope.

Prayer: Lord, help me to be even a little less arrogant today than I was yesterday. Help me to practice the humility of Christ, who did not seek to be served, but to give himself for others.

One Word: Practice humility.

December

Sun	Mon	Tue	Wed	Thu	Fri	Sat
					1	2
3	4	5	6	7	8	9
10	11	12	13	14	15	16
17	18	19	20	21	22	23
24	25	26	27	28	29	30
31						

GENEROSITY

Proverbs 11:16-31
Key Verse 11:25

Have you ever felt offended by another's careless words or actions and one thing led to another and a lot more damage occurred than ever imagined? You are not alone. We all make mistakes and have hurt others and have been hurt.

What if we believed that the offender was actually trying their very best, made an honest mistake, or were misunderstood? Trust is made stronger when we are generous rather than quick to condemn and point out faults. Being generous doesn't mean being a pushover, but it is being curious before accusing. It is responding with care rather than reacting. Even if people did wrong, a little generosity can leave open the possibility for restoration and reconciliation.

Jesus generously healed ten lepers, even though only one came back to thank him. Jesus fed, healed, and taught many regardless of whether they chose to follow him. Jesus invested in 12 disciples even though they would all abandon him in his most vulnerable moment. God gives generously and indiscriminately to all who seek him.

Prayer: Lord, help me to be generous in my relationship with others. Help me not to be quick to judge or condemn.

One Word: Be generous.

WORDS AND WORKS

Proverbs 12:1-14
Key Verse 12:14

We are filled not just by what goes into our mouths but what comes out of our mouths and into our ears and dwells in our hearts. What we say can destroy or build up others, so we must be careful to use our words thoughtfully and meaningfully. A kind and encouraging word can refresh a weary or anxious soul. A wise word can help someone learn and grow in wisdom. Brutal honesty is sometimes just brutal and not helpful, but words of love, sprinkled with humility, can build up others.

Sometimes, we long for an easy reward, such as working less and getting paid more. But no reward comes from idle hands. As God is constantly working (Jn 5:17), we must work to build a rewarding and blessed life, family, and community. We need to rest but avoid being idle and complacent. The kingdom of God advances when we are the hands and feet of Christ to the world. The harvest is plentiful, but the workers are few (Mat 9:37). What work is God calling me to do today?

Prayer: Lord, you fill us with good things. May we use our words and hands to build others up rather than tearing down.

One Word: Speak and work for good.

THE WAY OF LIFE

Proverbs 12:15-28
Key Verse 12:28

In the way of righteousness, there is life (28). Wisdom from God is not rocket science. You don't even need to have a college degree to receive it. Righteousness is about valuing and honoring life. Jesus came to give life to the full (Jn 10:10). There are many things that steal our joy. Although Jesus didn't come to rid the world of hardships, suffering, or injustice, he did come to be with us in our suffering and to give us hope and resurrection from the depth of sin and death.

Jesus came to us in our sickness, loss, and rejection that we may realize how much God cares for our life and to give us his grace so we, too, can live a life of love and compassion for others. We are Jesus' disciples when we love one another. When we know that God loves us, life always finds a way to blossom and grow even beyond the suffering and doom of the world. While some may build rockets to escape, we may find God's love and mercy to endure in our bodies and our communities in this world and beyond.

Prayer: Lord, your wisdom gives life to even the most lost causes. May we receive your wisdom that endures all the world's storms.

One Word: The way of life.

WISDOM: A FOUNTAIN OF LIFE

Proverbs 13:1-25
Key Verse 13:14

The impact of a person's speech (2,3), the fruit of hard work and diligence (4,11), and how the righteous live (5-6,9,21,25) are all discussed in this chapter. Underlying all these teachings is a person's attitude toward instruction and correction. Though we desire the positive results from the teachings of Proverbs, we are also sinful human beings. We naturally default to living according to our pride and feelings. How receptive are you to the instruction of those who are wiser than you?

Receiving instruction begins with a humble heart towards our Father's instruction and his rebukes at our foolishness (1), and this process continues throughout life. Pride brings strife (10a). Scorning instruction has negative consequences (13a). When we keep company with fools, surely harm, poverty, and shame will follow (18,20). However, when we humbly take advice from the wise, we ourselves grow in wisdom. Respecting a command (13b) and heeding correction (18b), especially from God's word, will bring reward and honor. We should surround ourselves with wise people.

The teaching of the wise gives life and turns us from death (14). This is ultimately fulfilled in Jesus Christ who has the words of eternal life (Jn 6:68). Will you humbly listen to Jesus today?

Prayer: Father, your word is a fountain of life. Give me an open heart to receive your instruction.

One Word: A right attitude toward wisdom.

GIVE THOUGHT TO YOUR STEPS

Proverbs 14:1-17
Key Verse 14:15

Knowledge and supposed wisdom are more abundant and accessible in the modern world than ever before. The latest technologies have made finding advice on almost any matter at any time and at anywhere possible. The amount of information is overwhelming in our world - but how can we know what is correct? How can we find true wisdom?

We start with humbly fearing the LORD (2,16,1:7, 3:5) and observing the fruit of wise people (1,3b,7). A mocker cannot find wisdom because of pride (6a). We also need discernment (6b) so that we do not live as the simpletons (15a) and those who follow worldly consensus do. For example, seeking riches and comfort seems to be common wisdom as we live our lives in the world, but in the end, it will lead to death (12, Lk 9:24-25).

Instead of living by worldly consensus or reacting to every advice or information that we receive, Proverbs encourages us to give thought to our ways (8a). We ought to carefully, and deliberately, give thought to the steps we are taking (15). When we give thought to our ways based on God's word and pray to God, he will give us the wisdom we need (Ja 1:5). Are the steps you are taking in life leading you toward a deeper relationship with God and others in love?

Prayer: Father, please give us discernment as we give thought to our steps and live with your wisdom.

One Word: Be thoughtful and pray.

THE LORD IS A SECURE FORTRESS

Proverbs 14:18-35
Key Verse 14:26

Whatever we have is a blessing from God. The author of Proverbs observes that the poor are shunned, even by those close to them, whereas the rich have friends (20). God's children do not reject and despise the poor. Doing so is a sin. Rather, we must be kind to the needy (21b). With wisdom, God's children work hard which leads to profit and wealth. Profit and wealth are kindnesses from God which we can use to show kindness to the poor and needy. This honors God and practically demonstrates how to love our neighbor as ourselves (31). God has blessed us with wealth – material, spiritual, love, time, opportunities, etc. Let us honor God with our wealth!

Yet, wealth cannot provide lasting refuge and security. Only the LORD is an eternally secure fortress for us and for our children (26). No amount of material wealth can save a person from death. But fearing the LORD is a fountain of life and can turn a person from the snares of death (27). The wicked are brought down when calamity strikes. But the LORD our God, even in death, is a refuge and strength for the righteous (32, Ps 46:1). Will you fully trust God to be your fortress and refuge?

Prayer: Father, thank you for being my true security and for being a refuge in times of trouble. Help me use what you've given to me to bless those who are in need.

One Word: God is my refuge and fortress.

SPEAK WITH WISDOM

Proverbs 15:1-17
Key Verse 15:2

Our words can have a powerful effect on others, for better or for worse. Words spoken gently can turn away wrath, but one harsh word can stir up anger (1). Therefore, the author of Proverbs encourages us to shape our words with wisdom. A wise person's speech makes seeking knowledge and wisdom attractive to others (2a). Wisdom directs a person to speak soothing words which can be a tree of life to a suffering person (4a).

In contrast, fools pour out folly with their words (2b) and even feed on that folly (14b). Their perverse words can crush a person (4b). In fact, the New Testament compares the tongue to a destructive fire to emphasize its potential for evil (Ja 3:6). Are your words full of wisdom that bring life to others - or do your words tear others down?

What we say comes from our hearts (Mt 15:18). The heart of a fool is not upright. But the heart of the wise is discerning (14a). A heart that is wise is a heart that fears the LORD and knows that love is better than wealth (16,17). Let us pray for a heart that is wise so that the words we speak may be full of godly wisdom and life.

Prayer: Father, please forgive my sins of speaking foolishness and hurting others with my words. Change my heart so that I may speak wisdom.

One Word: A wise tongue.

FEAR THE LORD

Proverbs 15:18-33
Key Verse 15:33

The book of Proverbs contains much wisdom meant to be applied to our everyday life. Whether the wisdom is about controlling our temper (18), not being lazy (19a), honoring our parents (20), or finding many advisers (22), these principles - when lived out - can have a positive impact on our life. However, Proverbs are intended for more than only bringing success in our earthly life. Putting into practice the wisdom of Proverbs can set our path of life on an upward trajectory, towards the LORD, instead of one that leads downwards, towards death (24).

True wisdom leads us to fear the LORD. This theme is repeated several times in Proverbs (1:7, 9:10, 15:33). To fear the LORD is to be humble before God (33). The LORD opposes the proud (25a) but honors the humble (33b). Those who are humble accept life-giving correction (31,32). The LORD knows our thoughts and detests the thoughts of the wicked (26a). He is far from the wicked (29a). The LORD protects widows from the schemes of the proud (25b). He is pleased when we speak gracious words. The LORD also hears the prayers of the righteous (29b).

Prayer: Father, thank you for the book of Proverbs. May your word direct my path toward you. Help me to know and fear you more.

One Word: Wisdom's instruction is to fear the LORD.

GOD ESTABLISHES PLANS

Proverbs 16:1-9
Key Verse 16:3

Planning out a course to achieve a goal or to get somewhere in life can be good and necessary. We frequently make plans, whether big or small. Our hearts form our plans. We may believe that our motives and ways are pure (2a). But we must also know and accept that God is sovereign over all our human plans. He knows our hearts and motivations better than ourselves. We must guard our hearts against pride (5). In the end, the outcome of our plans belongs to God.

Therefore, whatever we plan to do, we are encouraged to commit it to the LORD. The LORD is the one who establishes our plans and steps (3,9). This does not mean that the result will always be what we had originally planned or hoped. It means that we conform our plans and thoughts to God's plans and God's will. Our faith is in God, not our plans. Our faith is that the LORD works out everything to its proper end (4a). We trust that God works for the good of those who love him (Ro 8:28).

Will you invite God into your plans and seek his will? Will you, as a first priority, delight in the LORD and commit your plans to him? Then God will establish your plans and give you the desires of your heart (3, Ps 37:4-6).

Prayer: Father, thank you for establishing our plans and steps. Help me to commit my plans to you.

One Word: Commit to the LORD whatever you do.

PRIDE LEADS TO DESTRUCTION

Proverbs 16:10-33
Key Verse 16:18

Verses 10-15 teach us about just and upright kings. Their mouths do not betray justice (10). They detest wrongdoing and take pleasure in honest lips (11,12a). The throne of a good king is established in righteousness (12b). A king may have power over life and death (14b,15). We need wisdom to deal with those in power (14a). Let us pray for kings and rulers so that we may lead peaceful lives and be able to freely share the gospel (1 Ti 2:1-4).

The next set of Proverbs contrasts the value of wisdom and the dangers of pride. Wisdom is more valuable than gold. The wise are those who heed instruction. Such people prosper and are blessed (20). Wisdom or prudence is a fountain of life (23). Wise and gracious words are sweet to the soul and promote healing (24). However, pride is the greatest barrier to growing in wisdom from God. Pride rejects instruction. The fruit of pride is seen in a scoundrel (27), the perverse (28), the violent (29), and those who use deceit to plan evil (30). Proud and even haughty people may seem to get ahead in the world. But pride ultimately leads to destruction (18), and even death (25). Watch out for pride! Ask God daily for a humble heart that responds to his word.

Prayer: Father, please forgive my pride that insists on its own way. Thank you for your word, which grows me in wisdom. Please also help our rulers to honor you and govern with wisdom.

One Word: A haughty spirit before a fall.

A PROPHECY OF RESTORATION

Jeremiah 16:1-21
Key Verse 16:14-15

Jeremiah's unique mission was so difficult. The Lord told him not to marry or raise a family because of the terrible judgment coming on the land (1-2). Even the normal joys of life, such as eating and celebrating weddings, would not take place (8-9). We don't know if such things will happen in our nation and our time. But we are called to be a positive blessing to the people around us. Jesus attended many feasts because he came bearing good news of salvation, blessing those around him (Mt 9:11).

Even though Jeremiah's main message was one of judgment, God also gave him the message of restoration. God's work of bringing Israel back from exile would be as memorable as when he first brought them out of Egypt in Moses' time (14-15).

The gospel message is also a message of judgment for sin and restoration in Jesus. People are already suffering from the curse of their sins, but we are like fishermen whom Jesus sends to restore people to God from all corners of the earth (16). When we don't understand why God allows so much suffering, we should remember the hope of restoration.

Prayer: Father, thank you for the message of restoration that we can put our hope in even during judgment.

One Word: God restores after punishment.

TRUST IN THE LORD

Jeremiah 17:1-27
Key Verse 17:7

This passage offers two ways to live: by putting our trust and hope in people, or by depending on God. Putting our hope in people is the definition of a cursed life (5) because people cannot provide what our soul really needs. A life depending on people soon becomes like a spiritual desert (6). But God's abundant blessing is on those who trust in him, and they bear good fruit even when the world is troubled (7-8).

Our heart often deceives us with false sources of hope (9) because it's easier to rely on what we can see and touch. But God knows us inside and out (10), so we should pray to God and ask him to heal us from our sin-sickness, as Jeremiah did (14). Jeremiah was not perfect, and more than once he became seriously discouraged. But he was willing to be used as a shepherd by God (16), and God was faithful to him, delivered him from trouble, and used his life greatly. Through Jesus, we can have the same relationship with God that Jeremiah did. When we come to Jesus with faith, he heals us spiritually, forgiving all our sins, and he sets us apart for his good purpose.

Prayer: Father, thank you for showing me how deceitful my heart is, so I might come to you for grace and healing. May I also be used as your shepherd so others can receive healing in Jesus.

One Word: Heal me, Lord.

LIKE CLAY IN THE POTTER'S HANDS

Jeremiah 18:1-23
Key Verse 18:6

It is always fascinating to watch a potter working with a lump of clay. The potter spends much time carefully molding the clay into something beautiful. But if something goes wrong, the potter crushes his creation and starts over, making it into something else. The Lord brought Jeremiah to the potter's house so he could learn the lesson of the potter. Israel was the lump of clay, and the Lord was the potter. As the potter with clay, the Lord can do whatever he wants with his creation. He can build up or plant if he wills. He can also uproot and destroy at his will. Although Jeremiah warned the Lord's people of this, they were determined that they would not humble themselves before him. So, the Lord would crush them.

Sometimes the word of the Lord does not bring us comfort. Sometimes it goes against our own plans and desires. Jeremiah prophesied the true word of the Lord, but others didn't like it, so they sought to persecute him. In truth these people wanted to be their own gods. They didn't want to submit to the Lord. Jeremiah prayed to the Lord, putting his trust in his protection.

Prayer: Father, we are like clay, and you the potter. You are the sovereign Lord who molds us to your will. Help us repent and come to you that you may build us up.

One Word: We are in the Lord's hands.

THE VALLEY OF SLAUGHTER

Jeremiah 19:1-15
Key Verse 19:6

The Lord told Jeremiah to buy a clay jar and to take it, along with some of the elders of the people, to the Valley of Ben Hinnom. This was the place where some of the kings of Judah had practiced child sacrifice. There, Jeremiah was to proclaim disaster for Judah and Jerusalem. For the people of Judah and Jerusalem had forsaken the Lord. They had burned incense to other gods. Worst of all, they had shed the blood of innocent victims, even slaughtering children to appease foreign gods like Baal.

The Lord would judge them by giving them over to their enemies in that very place. The people of Judah and Jerusalem would be slaughtered. Their bodies would end up as food for the birds and wild animals. The city of Jerusalem would become a place of horror and scorn to the other nations. The siege their enemies would put them under would last so long the people of Jerusalem would engage in cannibalism to survive. The Lord's judgment on sin is truly a horrible thing!

After the warning given to the elders of the city, the Lord instructed Jeremiah to break the clay jar as symbolism for what would happen to the city. Then, Jeremiah returned to the city and warned the people of the impending disaster.

Prayer: Father, you are the Lord who judges the sin of the world. Help us to repent and turn to you.

One Word: God will punish sin.

HIS WORD IS IN MY HEART LIKE A FIRE

Jeremiah 20:1-18
Key Verse 20:9

Because of what Jeremiah was prophesying, he was beaten and arrested by Pashhur, a priest who was in charge of the temple of the Lord. Jeremiah was detained overnight, and upon release, he rebuked Pashhur, telling him the Lord had renamed him "Terror on Every Side." Pashhur had been prophesying words of comfort and victory over the Babylonians to the people of Judah, but the people of Judah, including Pashhur and all his family would be in terror when the Babylonians came. The Babylonians would devastate the city of Jerusalem, and take many into exile. Pashhur would never see his homeland again.

Jeremiah then turned to the Lord with a complaint. The word of the Lord burned within Jeremiah. He had to prophesy the words the Lord had given him. But his words brought him nothing but trouble and suffering from the hands of his countrymen. But Jeremiah could turn to the Lord as a mighty warrior, protecting him from all his enemies. Those trying to harm him would all fail. So, Jeremiah praised the Lord. Obedience to the Lord is sometimes painful. But we can always be assured He is with us.

Prayer: Father, your word is like a burning fire within me. Help me to speak your word to others with full assurance of you.

One Word: The Lord's word is a burning fire.

THE WAY OF LIFE AND THE WAY OF DEATH

Jeremiah 21:1-22:9
Key Verse 21:8

Judah was being attacked by the Babylonian king, Nebuchadnezzar. King Zedekiah had been set up as a vassal king, but he had rebelled against Nebuchadnezzar, so Judah was once again attacked by the Babylonian army. So, Zedekiah sent two priests, Pashhur and Zephaniah to the prophet Jeremiah to ask him to inquire of the Lord so that the Babylonians would withdraw.

The Lord sent back three messages. To Zedekiah, the Lord said He himself would fight against him in full fury and wrath. Many would die of hunger, plague or the sword. The remainder would be taken by Babylon. The Lord was judging them for their grievous sin. To the people, the Lord told them He was setting out two paths for them to follow: one which led to death and one which led to life. Those who surrendered to Babylon would live. Finally, to the house of Judah, the Lord told them to administer justice.

What is it to administer justice? Rescuing people from oppression, and refraining from violence against foreigners, widows, and orphans is what administering justice means. But they would not do so, for they had forsaken the way of the Lord.

Prayer: Father, thank you for setting before us the path to life. There is a path that looks easier, but this one leads to death. Help us to choose the harder path, knowing it will lead to life.

One Word: Take the way of life.

WHAT IT MEANS TO KNOW THE LORD

Jeremiah 22:10-23
Key Verse 22:16

Zedekiah was made a puppet king of Judah by King Nebuchadnezzar of Babylon. He did evil in the eyes of the Lord (2Ki 17:24). He was preceded by three other kings, all of whom also did evil in the eyes of the Lord. Shallum (Jehoahaz) was taken into Egypt by Pharaoh Necho and he died there. Next, Shallum's son, Jehoiakim, also did evil in the eyes of the Lord. He refused to recognize the Lord; nor did he heed the warnings of what happened to his father. He died in Jerusalem during the Babylonian invasion. No one mourned him when he died. His son, Jehoiachin, also did evil in the eyes of the Lord. He was carried off to Babylon and died there.

King Zedekiah had ample warning. He had the examples of his predecessors. He had been warned by Jeremiah to "do what is right." He was to turn away from unrighteousness and injustice. He was to do what was right and just—to defend the cause of the poor and needy, just as King David had done. We learn that is what it means to know God. Instead, Zedekiah was only set on dishonest gain, bloodshed, oppression and extortion.

Prayer: Father, it is so easy to chase after the things in this life. May I not forget about you, and may I do what is just and right, defending the cause of the poor and needy. In this, may I come to know you.

One Word: Do what is just and right; come to know God.

GOD WILL RAISE UP A RIGHTEOUS BRANCH

Jeremiah 22:24-23:8
Key Verse 23:5,6

God had no use for King Jehoiachin. The Lord said that, even if Jehoiachin was useful to him, he would still rid himself of him. He would deliver Jehoiachin into the hands of his enemies. Even his mother would be judged just as harshly. They would both be taken to a country not their own, and there they would die.

Then Jeremiah turned to the priests and other spiritual leaders of the nation. They were supposed to be shepherds of God's flock. They should have been helping those under their care to grow in faith in God. They should have been pointing the way to God. Instead, what they were doing was destroying and scattering the sheep of the Lord's pasture. Because they didn't bestow care on God's flock, the Lord would bestow punishment on them. They would be supplanted as shepherds for the Lord by others the Lord would raise up as he brought his people back from exile.

And in that day, the Lord would raise up from the line of David a righteous Branch. He would be a wise and just king. This king is Jesus. He is our Lord and our Righteous Savior.

Prayer: Father, thank you for Jesus, who you raised up as the Righteous Branch to save your people. Help us as a nation to turn to him and be saved.

One Word: God has raised up a Righteous Branch.

JUDGMENT AGAINST FALSE PROPHETS

Jeremiah 23:9-40
Key Verse 23:16

Because of false prophets, even the very land was cursed. Due to their corruption the land lay parched. They were adulterers and used their power unjustly. It was as Jesus told them—instead of bringing people to God, they ended up driving them away by their abuse. They prophesied in the name of Baal. They couldn't control their wickedness, even in the temple! They were like the people of Sodom and Gomorrah.

Therefore, the Lord would punish those prophets and priests who claimed to speak for God, but were speaking their own visions, dreams and messages. They would claim, "The Lord declares," when actually they were just speaking their own words. They were stealing the words of the Lord (30).

The words of men and women are powerless and give only false hope. The word of the Lord has the power to turn people from their evil ways. The word of the Lord is like fire and a hammer that breaks rocks into pieces. Similarly, it can break through our hardened hearts.

Prayer: Father, thank you for your word that gives life. Father, it is your word which gives life. Please raise up men and women who correctly handle the word of truth. Help us to hear your word and obey it.

One Word: Live by God's word, not man's.

GOOD AND BAD FIGS

Jeremiah 24:1-10
Key Verse 24:7

After the Babylonian invasion and the exile to Babylon of King Jehoiachin and many skilled workers and craftsmen, the Lord sent a vision to Jeremiah. The vision was of two baskets of figs; one containing figs that looked very good and delicious looking, the other with figs that were rancid and could not be eaten.

At that time, there were two groups of Judeans: those who were exiled to Babylon, and those who remained in Jerusalem. Many of the remnant of Jerusalem thought of going to Egypt for safety. With this context we can understand that the good figs were those who obeyed the Lord, surrendered to the Babylonians and were taken into exile. The Lord would bless them. He would watch over them for their good and prosper them. Then he would bring them back in his time. He would give them a heart that seeks him whole-heartedly.

On the other hand, the bad figs represented the evil King Zedekiah and others that remained in Jerusalem, in disobedience to the Lord's words. The Lord would make them abhorrent to all the other nations. Because they didn't obey the Lord, he would destroy them with sword, plague and famine. The Lord, not Egypt, was their sanctuary.

Prayer: Father, help us to turn to you with our whole hearts. Give us hearts to know you, that we may be your people, and you may be our God.

One Word: Come to God; be like a good fig.

YOUR PRAYER HAS BEEN HEARD

Luke 1:5-25
Key Verse 1:13

At this time Judea was ruled by Herod. Zechariah and Elizabeth were descended from the priestly line of Aaron, and they maintained a life of obedience to God and his word, but they were childless into their old age. So, whether at a national or a personal level, it might seem that the Lord was absent. This was the very time the Lord appeared. Zechariah was called to be a prayer servant for the nation. There an angel appeared to him. The Lord would answer his prayer, not only for the nation, but also for a son. The Lord was coming, and he would use John the Baptist as a source of joy for the people of Israel, to prepare them for the coming of the Lord. Outwardly the times looked dark, but the Lord was present and fulfilling his purpose, answering those who prayed so faithfully.

Zechariah could not believe what he saw and heard. Then the angel Gabriel struck him with silence until John's birth. The Lord was coming to fulfill his word at the appointed time. When Elizabeth became pregnant, she prayed and saw that the Lord shows his favor and takes away the disgrace of his people.

Prayer: Lord, the world looks dark. Help me to pray until I can see the Lord who shows favor and takes away disgrace. Make me a person prepared for the Lord.

One Word: The Lord answers prayer.

THE HIGHLY FAVORED ONE

Luke 1:26-38
Key Verse 1:38

When Mary heard that she had found favor with God, she was afraid and troubled. She must have known that God's favor--his grace--though beautiful, is costly. She was just a simple country girl who was engaged to a young man named Joseph. Joseph was a humble carpenter, but the blood of kings flowed in his veins, for he was a descendant of David. Mary was looking forward to their sweet home. But God had a mission for her. He had chosen her to be the mother of his Son Jesus, the promised Messiah who would rule over an eternal kingdom. God was sending his Son, Mary's son, to be the Savior of the world.

Mary did not hesitate because of the personal sacrifice involved; she hesitated because what God asked of her defied her human reason: it seemed impossible. But nothing is impossible with God. The angel told her about Elizabeth. And Mary made a decision of faith to give up her human dream and be totally available to God--to be the Lord's servant.

Prayer: Lord, let me serve you in any way you choose. Teach me to bear your costly grace.

One Word: I am the Lord's servant.

MY SPIRIT REJOICES

Luke 1:39-66
Key Verse 1:46-47

Upon hearing the angel's words, Mary rushed to Elizabeth. Elizabeth, filled with the Holy Spirit, saw Mary as the mother of her Lord. Even the baby in her womb leaped for joy.

Then Mary sang a song of praise. She deeply accepted the Lord's salvation work promised, saying, "My spirit rejoices in God my Savior." Her joy is the revelation of God. He is eternal and mighty, yet full of mercy for the humble. He is the God of history, especially Israel's history, and he is eternally faithful to his promises. He is joy for our spirits because he is our Savior.

Elizabeth gave birth, and everyone shared her joy. When it came time to name the baby, Zechariah was obedient to the Lord's command through the angel. He insisted on naming him John. He believed the Lord, and now his mouth was opened to praise God and to bring others to praise him as well.

Prayer: Lord, you are my source of joy. Use me to proclaim your saving grace and be a source of joy for others.

One Word: Rejoice in God our Savior.

ZECHARIAH'S SONG OF PRAISE

Luke 1:67-80
Key Verse 1:68

When Zechariah could speak again, it was through the Holy Spirit. He saw what God had already done. He has come to redeem his people. He has raised up a horn of salvation for them as he promised. He was faithful to his word through the prophets to raise up David's descendant as king, and he was faithful to the covenant he made with the patriarchs. When Zechariah saw the birth of his son, John, the Holy Spirit gave him prophetic insight to see and speak of the fulfillment of God's history, who has redeemed us from a hopeless world to the hope of eternal salvation.

In this context, Zechariah could speak of his son. He would serve the purpose of the Most High. He would prepare the people to hear and believe and accept the salvation provided to them, to know God's tender mercy and the light of life. God was pouring out his mercy. From childhood, John would grow as a servant to guide God's people in the path of peace—to proclaim his salvation.

Prayer: Lord, thank you for your faithfulness. Bless me with your Spirit, that I may proclaim your salvation work with assurance.

One Word: He has redeemed his people.

A SAVIOR HAS BEEN BORN TO YOU

Luke 2:1-14
Key Verse 2:11

Outwardly the world appeared to be ruled by Caesar Augustus and Rome. So, when the Roman ruler decided to take a census, everyone had to comply. Even though Mary was full term in her pregnancy, she and Joseph had to travel to Joseph's hometown of Bethlehem. There were no exceptions. Suddenly the time came for the baby to be born. It might seem like everything was ruled by worldly powers or happenstance, but this was God's doing, according to his promise. Jesus came to be born in this world and in this way. The world had no room for him. This all happened by God's sovereign will. He is the ruler of all.

The birth of the baby was announced to hard working shepherds as they tended their flocks. A host of angels appeared to them from heaven. They were terrified, but it was to these shepherds that the Lord made his glory known. The Savior of the world had come as a baby lying in a manger. He is glory to God and peace to men. He comes to lift us out of the rule of a cruel world to have peace and joy. He is the Savior born to us. He is good news from God.

Prayer: Lord, thank you for sending Jesus as a baby in a manger. Bless me with his peace and joy today.

One Word: Jesus is good news.

"BECAUSE YOU HAVE NOT LISTENED..."

Jeremiah 25:1-14
Key Verse 25:7

Jeremiah faithfully preached the word of God for twenty-three years. But God's own people, Judah, never listened. No matter how many prophets the Lord sent, Judah always turned a deaf ear to His word. So, the Lord himself warned them again, through the prophet Jeremiah. The Lord promised them that if they turned from their wicked ways, they would be able to stay in the land forever and ever. And he would never harm them. When we listen to the Lord, we are blessed indeed!

But because they did not listen to the Lord, he was angry with them. He would judge them and punish them and would bring harm to them. The Lord would use King Nebuchadnezzar of Babylon as his tool for judgment. He would completely destroy Judah and send the people into exile.

But the Lord also promised mercy on his people. After seventy years, the Lord would relent and turn and punish their captors for their own sin. He would do to Babylon what he did to Judah.

Prayer: Father, thank you for your mercy on sinners. Thank you that your wrath lasts only a brief time and that after your punishment comes blessings. Help us to listen to you at all times.

One Word: Listen to the Lord and obey!

THE CUP OF GOD'S WRATH

Jeremiah 25:15-38
Key Verse 25:29

In a vision, the Lord told Jeremiah to take the cup of God's wrath and to go to all the other nations on earth and make their leaders drink from the cup. So, Jeremiah obeyed the Lord. He travelled from nation to nation and made their leaders drink from the cup of the Lord's wrath. The Lord is God of all nations, not just Israel. All people have sinned against the Lord and are thus under the judgment and wrath of God. No one could escape, not even those who refused to drink from the cup. Even the shepherds would not be spared. They too fell under the wrath of God. All would be subject to the sword.

All have sinned and fallen short of the glory of God. And the wages of sin is death. We all deserve to fall by the sword of God's wrath for we have all sinned. But God sent Jesus to be an atoning sacrifice for our sins. Because of him, when the Lord sees us, he doesn't see a sinner. We are made white as snow because of Jesus' blood. We are forgiven and no longer under God's wrath.

Prayer: Father, we all deserve to drink from the cup of your wrath. We have all sinned against you. But Jesus took the cup and drank of it for us, so we are no longer under your wrath. Thank you, Jesus!

One Word: Jesus drank from the cup for me.

PERHAPS THEY WILL LISTEN...

Jeremiah 26:1-24
Key Verse 26:3

God had hope for his people that they would hear the word of the Lord and repent and turn from their wicked ways. So, he sent Jeremiah to the temple court to speak the word of the Lord. He told Jeremiah to speak the whole word of God and not to omit a single word. When Jeremiah spoke the whole words of God, the priests and the prophets wanted to see him executed. Instead of listening and repenting, they wanted to execute God's messenger. But Jeremiah was unfazed. He again spoke the message of listening and repenting. There were some godly men there who spoke up and saved Jeremiah from execution.

The word of the Lord is not popular. It convicts us of our sin and urges us to repent. Many times, when we speak the word of the Lord, people become angry with us. In some parts of the world, people are executed for speaking his word. But the Bible is full of examples of the Lord calling His people to speak His word boldly. He called Jeremiah to do so. He calls us to do so too.

Prayer: Father, your word is not always popular. It makes people uncomfortable because it confronts us with sin. Have mercy on us and help us to listen to your word and repent.

One Word: Listen to the word of the Lord!

GOD GIVES THE EARTH TO WHO HE PLEASES

Jeremiah 27:1-22
Key Verse 27:5,6

The Lord sent Jeremiah out with a yoke around his neck. The Lord told Jeremiah to go to the envoys of the kings of Moab, Ammon, Tyre and Sidon and to give them the word of the Lord to take back to their kings. The word was a forceful message that the Lord is the Creator God, creator of the heavens and all the earth. He can do with His creation what He wills. All these nations would soon be given into the hands of the King of Babylon. They would be subject to him for a time, until the time the Lord set for the Babylonians to be judged. Then, the Babylonians would be subjugated by others. If those nations refused to serve Babylon, the Lord would send the sword and plague to destroy them.

The same message was given to the nation of Judah. Jeremiah gave the word of the Lord to them, "Bow your neck under the yoke of the king of Babylon; serve him and his people and you will live." The Lord had a time set for the judgment of his people Judah. They would serve the king of Babylon for seventy years, until the time the Lord set for bringing His people out and leading them back to their homes. The message was as hard for Jeremiah to give as it was for the people to hear! But this word had to be spoken.

Prayer: Father, you are God who is sovereign over all things and all people everywhere. Help people around the world to come to know and acknowledge your sovereignty.

One Word: God gives to anyone he pleases.

A FALSE PROPHET AND A TRUE PROPHET

Jeremiah 28:1-17
Key Verse 28:15

This chapter contrasts two prophets. Hananiah was a false prophet. Jeremiah was a true prophet. Hananiah was a false prophet because he spoke false words. He said that the Lord had told him that within two years, He would throw the yoke of the king of Babylon off the necks of the people of Judah. Furthermore, the Lord would also bring back all the articles the Babylonians had carried from the Lord's house and had taken to Babylon. The Lord was also to bring back Jehoiachin, the King of Judah, who had been taken to Babylon.

Jeremiah said, "Amen!" to Hananiah's message. It would indeed be a great thing if what Hananiah spoke was true. But then Jeremiah pointed out that Hananiah's message contradicted all who came before him. A prophet cannot be considered a true prophet unless his word comes true.

Jeremiah didn't say anything else until the Lord gave him a message to give to Hananiah. The wooden yoke would be turned into an iron one. King Nebuchadnezzar's rule would be like an iron yoke around the neck of Judah. And because Hananiah spoke the false word of the Lord, he would die.

Prayer: Father, sometimes your word is hard to tell others because it sounds harsh, and the people don't like to hear it. Give me the courage to speak your word truly, as Jeremiah did.

One Word: Speak God's word truthfully.

YOUR MAKER IS YOUR HUSBAND

Isaiah 54:1-8
Key Verse 54:5

Sing, enlarge the place of your tent, and fear not! These are the commands of God for the people of Israel. In the Old Testament, the relationship between God and the nation Israel is compared to that of a husband and wife. Unfortunately, though, Israel had cheated in this marriage by worshiping other gods. As a result, they would be sent into captivity in Babylon and experience much shame and disgrace. However, God commanded them to sing because this was not the end of their relationship. They could sing because he promised to multiply their offspring. God commanded them to enlarge the place of their tent because he would restore their inheritance and expand their territory. They would possess the nations and populate the desolate cities. Furthermore, they were to fear not because God would completely remove their shame and disgrace. Their situation was hopeless, but God was their husband and he would redeem them. Israel suffered His wrath and anger for a brief time, but his love and compassion are forever.

What a tremendous reversal of fortune! If the Lord is your husband, what do you have to fear? What do you have to be ashamed of? You can rest in the hands of your Maker and Redeemer. It is time for you to sing and rejoice in him as well.

Prayer: *Father, your love and mercy never end.*

One Word: *The LORD is your Redeemer.*

Made in the USA
Monee, IL
26 September 2023

43483478R00059